THE CATHOLIC UNIVERSITY OF AMERICA
CANON LAW STUDIES
No. 306

THE PROBATION IN SOCIETIES OF QUASI-RELIGIOUS

A Historical Synopsis and a Commentary

BY
JOSEPH L. WATERS, S.S.J., J.C.L.
PRIEST OF THE SOCIETY OF ST. JOSEPH OF THE SACRED HEART

A DISSERTATION

SUBMITTED TO THE FACULTY OF THE SCHOOL OF CANON LAW OF THE CATHOLIC UNIVERSITY OF AMERICA IN PARTIAL FULFILLMENT OF THE REQUIREMENTS FOR THE DEGREE OF DOCTOR OF CANON LAW

THE CATHOLIC UNIVERSITY OF AMERICA PRESS
WASHINGTON, D. C.
1951

Imprimi Potest:
THOMAS P. McNAMARA, S.S.J.
Superior Generalis
Nihil Obstat:
HIERONYMOUS D. HANNAN, A.M., LL.B., S.T.D., J.C.D.
Censor Deputatus

Imprimatur:
✠ PATRICIUS A. O'BOYLE, D.D.
Archiepiscopus Washingtoniensis
Washingtonii, die 16 decembris, 1950.

MURRAY & HEISTER—WASHINGTON, D. C.
PRINTED IN THE UNITED STATES OF AMERICA

TO MY MOTHER
AND
IN MEMORY OF
MY FATHER

TABLE OF CONTENTS

PART ONE

HISTORICAL SYNOPSIS

FOREWORD

Since the day when Our Blessed Lord first invited His listeners, " Come, follow Me," countless men and women have turned their backs upon worldly pursuits and followed in the steps of the Master. The Kingdom of God and the kingdom of the world were, to them, two opposites, and they chose to cast their lot with Christ.

Since man has a social nature, these souls with kindred minds soon banded together into communities with definite rules and exercises. This was the beginning of the religious life. By a process of evolution, the basic elements of the religious life became clearly defined. These are: a stable manner of life, approval of the Holy See, and the profession of the three public vows of poverty, chastity and obedience.

It is in this last element that the societies of " Quasi-religious " differ from the religious strictly so-called. Although the members of such societies follow, to some extent, the mode of life of the religious, they are bound together only by private vows, or an oath, or a promise, or by no juridic bond at all, and hence they cannot be properly called religious.[1]

It was not until the later Middle Ages that the first of these societies came into existence. In the centuries that followed they have held an honorable place in the life of the Church and have increased in number and importance. In the United States alone at least sixteen such communities are represented. The fact that they are not bound by the rigidity of the religious life has enabled them to engage in works in which religious institutes could labor only with difficulty.

As Fr. Creusen remarks,[2] a student of the legislation governing such societies is amazed at the extreme rarity of legal sources, which is even more remarkable when one considers the lengthy history of such organizations. An explanation may, perhaps, be

[1] Can. 673.

[2] " Sociétés Réligieuses," *Ephemerides Theologicae Lovanienses* (Brugis: Beyaert, 1924 ——), XI (1934), 778–786.

found in the fact that, because of the essential distinction between religious institutes and quasi-religious societies, the many documents which developed the legislation governing religious were not applicable to societies without vows; moreover, their simplified organization, the absence of privileges and the diocesan character of many of them entailed less frequent recourse to the Holy See.

This dissertation is an attempt to study the probationary period in quasi-religious societies. It has been felt best to study the idea of a period of probation in the early ages of the Church, to examine its development in the later ages, and finally to inquire into the existence of, provisions for and nature of the probationary period in quasi-religious societies.

The writer wishes to express his gratitude to the Very Rev. Thomas P. McNamara, S.S.J., Superior General of the Society of Saint Joseph, and to the Very Rev. Edward V. Casserly, S.S.J., Vicar General of the Society, for the opportunity to pursue advanced studies in Canon Law; to the Faculty of the School of Canon Law of The Catholic University of America for their guidance and direction; and to all others who have in any way, by interest and by active aid, contributed to the preparation of this dissertation.

PART 1—HISTORICAL SYNOPSIS

CHAPTER I

EARLY DEVELOPMENT OF THE NOVITIATE

The development of the canonical institution of the novitiate has followed closely the evolution of the religious life itself. As the religious life has evolved into ever more perfect forms, so too has the novitiate had a comparable development. For this reason it will be necessary to treat in a brief manner the growth and diffusion of the religious life, as well as the concept of a probationary period.

Christ, by His example, taught the religious life and invited all who wished to strive after perfection to embrace it.[1] The Apostles followed the example and doctrine of Christ as a rule of life and they were joined in this by many of the early Christians, who, besides accepting the Commandments, also followed the counsels of Our Lord, particularly poverty.[2]

From the earliest ages of the Church there were Christians who added the external mortification of fasting, abstinence and other penances to internal abnegation, so that by castigating their bodies they might reduce them to subjection. Those who devoted themselves to these prayers, privations and other works were called *ascetae,* a word borrowed from the ancient athletes.[3] They distributed their goods to the poor, abstained from all worldly business, and lived as solitaries. They lived their lives in chastity and perfect continence, often with a perpetual vow to that effect.[4] For the most part they remained in their own homes, but lived apart from their families. They constituted a definite order or

---

[1] Matt., XIX, 21.

[2] Acts, II, 44–45; IV, 32–36.

[3] Steiger, "De propagatione et diffusione vitae religiosae," *Periodica de Re Canonica et Morali utilia praesertim Religiosis et Missionariis* (Brugis, 1920–1927), XIII (1924), (57) (hereafter cited *Periodica*).

[4] Justinus, *Apologia I,* c. 15 et 29—Migne, *Patrologiae Cursus Completus, Series Graeca* (161 vols., Parisiis, 1857–1866), VI, 350–374 (hereafter cited *MPG*).

class, midway between the clergy and the laity, and at sacred functions were preceded only by the clergy. Even after the introduction of monachism, this class of the *ascetae* continued to exist for many centuries.

A. Development in the East

1. *The Novitiate among the Early Hermits*

In the middle of the third century a new kind of *ascetae* came into being. With the outbreak of the Decian persecution (250) many Christians fled to the mountain regions and deserts of Egypt. Their numbers were augmented in consequence of the persecution of the Emperor Diocletian (303). Many of those who had fled to the desert at the outbreak of these persecutions were attracted by the sweetness of the contemplative life and elected to remain there when the persecutions had ceased. There were also others who had fled to the desert, not to escape persecution, but to serve God more freely. These latter were the founders of the eremitical life. The first of these was Saint Paul (228–341), who is justly called the "First Hermit."[5]

It was Saint Anthony of Egypt (ca. 251–356) who first organized the numerous hermits living in Upper Egypt and guided them in the monastic life. The monachism that Saint Anthony taught was eremitical in character, and its dominating principle was a spirit of individualism.[6] These monks often lived in the same place, but were not bound together by a common rule or by exercises in common.[7] Saint Athanasius (295–373), in his *Vita S. Antonii,* quoted an entire discourse in which the "Father of Christian Monks" offered an outline of all his teaching.[8] The discipline which he imposed on his disciples was practically all of a spiritual and ascetic nature. Saint Anthony did not write a

---

[5] Steiger, "De propagatione et diffusione vitae religiosae," *Periodica,* XIII (1924), (44).

[6] Cuthbert Butler, *Benedictine Monachism* (London: Longmans, Green and Co., 1919), p. 12.

[7] F. Cayré, *Manual of Patrology and History of Theology* (translated by H. Howitt, 2 vols., Tournai: Desclée and Co., 1936–1940), I, 502.

[8] *Vita S. Antonii—MPG,* XXVI, 838–976.

Rule, and that which is attributed to him, and is followed by monks of the Maronite Rite, is of a later age.[9]

A reading of the *Vita* of Saint Anthony gives no indication that there was a formal probationary period among the Antonian monks. However, Palladius (ca. 365–ca. 430) related[10] that Saint Anthony refused admission to Paul the Simple (+ ca. 339) until the latter had persevered four days in standing outside the door of Anthony's cell. He finally admitted Paul on the condition that the latter would follow his commands. Anthony then subjected the disciple to a long period of trials, which lasted for at least several weeks. It was only after he had successfully surmounted these trials that Paul was finally admitted to the monastic life.

It seems from this that, even though there was no formal period of probation, membership in the group of Antonian monks was not given until the candidate had successfully undergone a series of tests to prove his power of perseverance and his worthy intentions.

2. *The Novitiate among the Early Cenobites*

The cenobitical type of monasticism was established by Saint Pachomius (292–346). About 318 Pachomius settled upon one of the islands formed by the Nile, at Tabennisi, and there founded a community life characterized by submission to a Rule and a recognition of true superiors. Thanks to firm disciplinary measures, he was able to gather together several hundred cenobites in a single monastery, and other houses were soon founded and united under the authority of a supreme superior. About the year 400, the institute had attracted nearly 5000 monks.[11] Most remarkable of all was the fact that the group of Pachomian monks immediately took shape as a fully organized congregation, with a supreme superior, a system of visitations, and all the machinery of

[9] Steiger, "De propagatione et diffusione vitae religiosae," *Periodica*, XIII (1924), (45).

[10] Palladius, *Historia Lausiaca*, c. 28—Migne, *Patrologiae Cursus Completus, Series Latina* (221 vols., Parisiis, 1844–1864), LXXIII, 1127 (hereafter cited *MPL*).

[11] Cayré, *Manual of Patrology and History of Theology*, I, 504.

a centralized government, such as does not again appear in the monastic world until the rise of the Cistercians and the Mendicant Orders eight or nine centuries later.[12]

The Rule of Saint Pachomius, written in Coptic about 315, is preserved in Saint Jerome's translation, made in about the year 404.[13] The 49th Chapter of the *Regula Pachomii* thus set forth the requirements for admission to the community:

> Si quis accesserit ad ostium monasterii, volens saeculum renuntiare et fratrum aggregari numero, non habebit intrandi libertatem, sed prius nuntiabitur Patri monasterii, et manebit paucis diebus foris ante januam, et docebitur orationem Dominicam ac psalmos, quantos poterit ediscere; et diligenter sui experimentum dabit, ne forte mali quidpiam fecerit, et turbatus ad horam timore discesserit, aut sub aliqua potestate sit; et utrum possit renuntiare parentibus suis, et propriam contemnere facultatem. Si enim viderint aptum ad orationem et ad omnia, tunc docebitur et reliquas monasterii disciplinas quas servare debeat et facere, quibusque servire, sive in collecta omnium fratrum, sive in domo cui tradendus est, sive in vescendi ordine; ut instructus et perfectus in omni opere bono, fratribus copuletur. Tunc nudabunt eum vestimentis saecularibus et induent habitu monachorum, tradentque ostiario, ut orationis tempore adducat eum in conspectu omnium fratrum: sedebitque in loco in quo ei praeceptum fuerit. Vestimenta autem, quae secum detulerat, accipient qui huic rei propositi sunt, et inferent in repositorium et erunt in potestate principis monasterii.[14]

It seems, from this chapter in the Pachomian Rule, that two separate periods of probation were required, corresponding to our present-day postulancy and novitiate. In the first period the candidate was subjected to an examination from which was to be determined the sincerity of his desire to embrace the cenobitic life. Cassian (ca. 360–ca. 433) indicated that this period lasted for ten

[12] *The Catholic Encyclopedia* (15 vols., with Index and 2 Supplements, New York, 1907–1922), s. v. "Monasticism," X, 462.

[13] *S. Eusebii Hieronymi Translatio Latina Regulae Sancti Pachomii—MPL,* XXIII, 61–86.

[14] *Regula Pachomii—MPL,* XXIII, 70.

days,[15] but the Rule itself did not determine the exact duration of this period, since it stated merely that the candidate was to remain outside the door of the monastery for a few days. After this preliminary probation, the aspirant, if judged suitable, was admitted to the monastery and was taught the Rule and the monastic mode of life, so that "*instructus atque perfectus in omni opere bono, fratribus copuletur.*" [16] This appears to correspond to the modern novitiate. The *Regula* did not indicate how long this probationary period was to last. Cassian stated that it lasted for an entire year.[17] Palladius, in his *Historia Lausiaca,*[18] and Sozomen (ca. 400– + after 450), in his *Historia Ecclesiastica,*[19] were both of the opinion that the period of trial lasted for three years. Dionysius Exiguus, who in 530 made a translation of the *Life of Saint Pachomius* which had been written by a Greek author who was a contemporary of the Saint,[20] interpreted the Rule in this manner:

> Qui vero semel in hoc intraret monasterium, ut ibi jugiter permaneret, per tres annos a studiis sacratioribus arceretur, operaretur opera sua simpliciter, et ita post triennium stadium certaminis introiret.[21]

However, one of the foremost students of Pachomian monasticism, Ladeuze (1870–1940), completely rejected the notion of the existence of a novitiate in the monasteries of Saint Pachomius, and was of the opinion that the first admission into the community was definitive. In support of his contention he cited several instances in which candidates were admitted though they had not

---

15 *De Institutis Coenobiorum: Collationes XXIV,* Lib. IV, cap. 3—*Corpus Scriptorum Ecclesiasticorum Latinorum* (Editum consilio et impensis Academiae Litterarum Caesereae Vindobonensis, Vindobonae: apud Geroldi Filium, 1866 ——), XVII, Pars I, 49–50 (hereafter cited *CSEL*).

16 *Regula Pachomii—MPL,* XXIII, 70.

17 *De Institutis Coenobiorum,* Lib. IV, cap. 7—*CSEL,* XVII, Pars I, 52.

18 C. 38—*MPL,* LXXIII, 1137–1138.

19 Lib. III, c. 14—*MPL,* LXVII, 1071.

20 *Vita Sancti Pachomii, auctore Graeco incerto, interprete Dionysio Exiguo Abbate Romano—MPL,* LXXIII, 231–272.

21 *Vita Sancti Pachomii—MPL,* LXXIII, 242.

undergone any period of trial other than for the few days during which they stood outside the door of the monastery.[22]

He stated that the absence of a novitiate was supplied for by means of the examination preliminary to admission, through the power given to the superior to dismiss those whose conduct was disedifying, and in view of the special watchfulness and extraordinary exercises to which the Saint subjected those whose virtue was open to question. This last point could be regarded as a substitute for the novitiate, but the fact that it was necessary to introduce a special trial for particular individuals points out the fact that the novitiate did not exist among the Pachomian monks as a regular and general institution.

3. *The Early Cenobites as Forerunners of Quasi-Religious*

Nowhere, either in the *Lives* or in the different versions of the Rule of Saint Pachomius, was there any mention of vows. When the Saint found it necessary to correct a fault, he used moral considerations derived either from the usefulness of his Rule or from the seriousness of the fault that had been committed. But he never appealed to any vow that the subject had taken before God. Certainly the Pachomian institutes led, as an almost inevitable result, to the adoption of perpetual vows. But Pachomius himself never made religious vows a part of his concept of the religious life. Among his monks there existed simply the agreement to observe all the rules, an agreement which was naturally linked to entrance into the religious life. Hence there was found in the Pachomian monasteries a parallel to the present-day communities of quasi-religious, whose members take no public vows, but live the common life, bound to their community by a promise or *propositum*.

The Pachomian Rule was followed, but with certain modifications, in the monasteries of Schenute (333–451). In them there was a greater austerity in the use of food, and longer periods of prayer and a stricter discipline were observed.[23] In place of the implicit promise made by the Pachomian monks on their

---

[22] Paulin Ladeuze, *Étude sur le Cénobitisme Pakhômien dans le IVe siècle et la Première Moitié du Ve* (Louvain: Typ. J. van Linthout, 1898), pp. 281–282.

[23] Cayré, *Manual of Patrology and History of Theology,* I, 505.

entrance into religion, Schenute demanded of his subjects an explicit promise of fidelity to the Rule. This was one more step toward the establishment of religious vows, but the monks of Schenute could not properly be called religious in the modern sense, so that they too could be grouped with the communities of quasi-religious.[24]

4. *The Novitiate in the Rule of Saint Basil*

Saint Basil (330–379) is known as the "Lawgiver of Eastern Monasticism." Born in Caesarea in Cappadocia, he established, about 359, a community of monks in a monastery near Neo-Caesarea. He was soon joined by many fervent Christians who also aspired to perfection.

About 360 he composed the Longer Rules to aid his monks in their aspirations towards perfection.[25] These did not constitute a monastic Rule in the ordinary sense of the word, but rather a synopsis of fifty-five lectures which treated the most important aspects of the religious life according to the Scriptures. They elaborated principles which were of capital importance, for it was on these principles that the monastic life in Cappadocia and Roman Asia was built up. The Shorter Rules, which numbered three hundred and thirteen, constituted a series of answers to questions on the religious life, and dealt chiefly with applications of principles.[26] A Latin translation of these Rules, made by Rufinus (ca. 345–410), was adopted by some Western monasteries.[27]

The Tenth *Interrogatio* of the Longer Rule prescribed the conditions for admission into the monasteries of Saint Basil. The aspirant was to be first subjected to an examination regarding his past life, his character and his ability to bear the burdens of the religious life. Even those who were of unstable habits or of questionable morals were not to be immediately dismissed, but rather to be subjected to suitable spiritual exercises, so that "*temporis progressu ac laboriosis exercitiis*" the superior would

---

[24] Cans. 487; 488, 1°; 673.

[25] *Regulae Fusius Tractatae—MPG,* XXXI, 889–1051.

[26] *Regulae Brevius Tractatae—MPG,* XXXI, 1051–1306.

[27] *Regulae Sancti Basilii Episcopi Cappodociae ad Monachos—MPL,* CIII, 483–554.

be able to determine whether it was proper to admit them. Once admitted into the monastery, the candidates were to undergo further trials in the test of their humility and obedience. When these had been successfully passed, the candidate was to be numbered among those who had dedicated themselves to God.[28]

It appears that there can be no doubt regarding the existence of a novitiate in the Basilian monasteries, and it seems reasonable to conclude that the preparation, probation and emendation of life that Saint Basil insisted upon for all candidates was impossible of accomplishment within a short space of time, and that correspondingly the Basilian noviceship was quite lengthy.[29]

B. Development in the West

1. *The Canons Regular of Saint Augustine*

Saint Augustine (354–430), as Bishop of Hippo (396–430), introduced the common manner of life among the secular clergy. The manner of life which he prescribed for them is found in Sermons 305 and 306 "*De vita et moribus clericorum suorum.*" [30] This was not a Rule strictly so-called, but merely a plan which set forth the purposes, aims and general practices of Saint Augustine's community. There was no mention whatever of any period of probation.

The Canons Regular, under Saint Augustine's direction, lived together, ate at a common table, observed the cloister and renounced all private property. Whether or not the Canons Regular could be called religious is a point on which authors disagree. Some held that they took the three vows of religion; others deny this. Steiger [31] is of the opinion that the only vow taken by the Canons Regular was that of the common life. A canon in the *Decretum Gratiani,* which seems to imply that they also took a

---

[28] *Regulae Fusius Tractatae, Interrogatio X—MPG,* XXXI, 943.

[29] Bakalarczyk, *De Novitiatu,* The Catholic University of America Canon Law Studies, n. 36 (Washington, D. C.: The Catholic University of America, 1927), p. 19.

[30] *MPL, XXXIX,* 1568–1581.

[31] "De propagatione et diffusione vitae religiosae," *Periodica,* XIII (1924), (74).

vow of obedience, was declared to be spurious by the *Correctores Romani.*[32]

Thomassinus (1619–1695), on the other hand, held that the clerics of Saint Augustine did take the three religious vows.[33] He argued that if there was no mention of the vows of obedience, chastity and stability in the sermons of Saint Augustine, this resulted from the reason that the members of his community were priests, deacons and other clerics who were already bound by these vows by reason of the sacred Orders which they had received. In view of the varying opinions, it cannot be stated definitely that the Canons Regular of Saint Augustine were religious in the modern sense of the term, or that they should be classed as quasi-religious.

2. *The Novitiate in the Rule of Saint Benedict*

The religious life in the West received its greatest impetus with Saint Benedict of Nurcia (ca. 480–ca. 547), the "Father of Western Monasticism." Born at Nurcia in Italy, he renounced the world and the wealth and position of his family when only seventeen, and took refuge in a cave at Subiaco in the Sabine Mountains. There he lived as a hermit for several years, and established twelve monasteries for his followers, over which he ruled as Abbot. Driven by persecution from Subiaco, he settled at Monte Cassino in 529, where he erected a large monastery and wrote his famous Rule, which combined manual labor with ascetic practices. The wisdom with which the Saint wrote is evidenced by the fact that today, fourteen centuries later, the Rule is observed without substantial modification in all the Benedictine monasteries throughout the world.

Chapter 58 of the Benedictine Rule contains the provisions for the admission of candidates into the monastic life.[34] Saint Benedict warned that entrance into the religious life should not be too

[32] C. 11, C. XII, q. 1.

[33] Ludovicus Thomassinus, *Vetus et Nova Ecclesiae Disciplina* (10 vols., Mainz, 1787), Pars I, Lib. III, c. 3, n. 5.

[34] Butler, *Sancti Benedicti Regula Monasteriorum, Editio Critico-Practica* (2 ed., Friburgi Brisgoviae: Herder & Co., 1927), c. LVIII.

easily granted. He quoted the words of Saint John: "Test the spirits to see whether they are of God." [35] In accordance with the counsel of the Apostle, he prescribed that the candidate was to spend four or five days patiently knocking at the door of the monastery and humbly suffering any discourtesies which might be shown to him. In this requirement one finds a certain resemblance to the Rule of Saint Pachomius.[36]

Having successfully passed this test and having given proof of the sincerity of his intentions, the candidate was admitted into the monastery in order that he might spend a few days in the guest house. Afterwards he was conducted into the section reserved for the novices and, having given a promise of stability, was admitted into the novitiate. The novices did not mingle with the other members of the community, but they prayed, meditated, slept and ate apart from the monks of the community. One of the older monks had charge of the novices and was given the responsibility of molding their spiritual life. Saint Benedict directed that the novice master watch the novices closely and be particularly solicitous regarding their recitation of the Divine Office, their practice of the virtue of obedience, and their willingness to undergo trials.

After two months the Rule was to be read to the novice. If he no longer wished to persevere, he had complete liberty to depart. If his intention had remained firm, his novitiate continued. The Rule was again read to him six months later and, finally, at the end of the complete year of the novitiate. Having proved that he was a worthy candidate, and having considered all things carefully, the novice made his promise of obedience, was vested in the monastic habit, and was received into the community.

It has been shown in the foregoing that practically all the monastic Rules provided for some period of trial,[37] but the Rule of Saint Benedict was the first to make a provision which required a specific time period for the novitiate.

---

[35] I John, IV, 1.

[36] *Regula Pachomii—MPL,* XXIII, 70.

[37] The reader is also referred to the *Concordia Regularum Patrum* of Saint Benedict of Aniane (750–821)—*MPL,* CIII, 702–1380.

3. *Diffusion of the Benedictine Rule*

A reference in Mansi relates that the Benedictine Rule was approved and confirmed in 595 by the II Council of Rome under Pope Gregory I (590–604), but this is of doubtful authenticity.[38]

During the sixth and seventh centuries, the great monastic establishments of Ireland, then at the height of their vitality, sent forth a stream of missionaries to Continental Europe. The Irish monasteries in Gaul, Germany, Switzerland and Italy remained beacons of learning throughout the whole medieval period. Chief pioneer in this movement was St. Columban (ca. 543–615). The Rule drawn up by him was adopted in many monasteries, but it proved so stern that it gradually yielded place to the milder Rule of Saint Benedict, which was more compatible with a stabilized organization. The Celtic spirit gradually gave way to the Roman, and within two centuries the Benedictine Rule came into general use throughout Western Europe.

Regional councils of the time exhorted the monasteries within their jurisdictions to adopt the Rule of Saint Benedict. The Council of Autun (670) noted that "it is fitting that Abbots and monks teach and observe the Rule of St. Benedict."[39] A German Council held under the authority of Saint Boniface at Ratisbon or Augsburg in 742 decreed that "monks and women religious should strive to direct and govern their monasteries in accord with the Rule of the Holy Father Benedict."[40]

The Council of Mainz[41] and the II Council of Rheims,[42] both held in the year 813, again encouraged the monasteries to follow the Benedictine Rule. The Council of Chalon-sur-Saône, celebrated the same year, observed that "almost all the monasteries in this region live according to the Rule of Saint Benedict."[43]

From this it can be seen that the Benedictine Rule gradually

---

[38] Nota Severini Binii in Mansi, *Sacrorum Conciliorum Nova et Amplissima Collectio* (53 vols. in 60, Paris, Leipzig, Arnhem, 1901-1927), X, 477 (hereafter cited Mansi).

[39] Can. 15—Mansi, XI, 124. Translation by the writer.

[40] Can. 7—Mansi, XII, 367. Translation by the writer.

[41] Can. 11—Mansi, XIV, 68.

[42] Can. 9—Mansi, XIV, 78.

[43] Can. 22—Mansi, XIV, 98. Translation by the writer.

replaced all the earlier Rules and, in time, was observed almost everywhere in Western Europe. Consequently it is safe to conclude that by the eleventh century it was an almost universal custom in the Western Church for all aspirants to the monastic life to fulfill a novitiate period of one year.

CHAPTER II

LATER DEVELOPMENT OF THE NOVITIATE

A. Development in the East

1. *Civil Legislation*

In the East, Caesaro-Papism showed its influence on the monastic life. Some of the legislation in Justinian's great work pertained to certain aspects of the religious life. Among the laws was one which decreed that aspirants to the religious life were not to be indiscriminately received by the superiors of monasteries, but should undergo a trial period of three years. During this period they were to be considered as not yet worthy of the monastic habit, but were to wear the vesture and tonsure of lay people and pass their time in studying the sacred sciences. At the end of this three-year period, if they had shown themselves to be of suitable and persevering temperament, and if they had received the approval of their superiors, they could be invested in the monastic habit.[1]

Elsewhere in Justinian's legislation there were found provisions for slaves who desired to embrace the religious life. If they persevered throughout the entire three-year period and were received into the community, they gained their liberty ("*vindicentur in liberatatem*").[2]

2. *Ecclesiastical Legislation*

The IV General Council of Constantinople (869) has given us the first *general* law which specifically determined the time of probation in the novitiate. The Council decreed that a three-year period was necessary, but permitted this to be reduced to six

1 *Corpus Iuris Civilis* (3 vols., Berolini: apud Weidmannos), Vol. III, ed. stereotypa quinta, *Novellae,* quas recognovit Rudolfus Schoell, absolvit Guglielmus Kroll, 1928; N. (5, 2).

2 N. (5, 5); N. (123, 35).

months in certain instances. It should be noted that this general law had a binding force only in the Eastern Church.[3]

B. Development in the West

In the letters of Pope Gregory I (590–604), who had been a Benedictine monk before his elevation to the Papacy, several references are found to matters pertaining to the novitiate. These were private responses and did not have the nature of general law.

In a letter to Eusebius, Urbicus and other abbots, he warned them that they were not to receive soldiers into their monasteries until they had weighed the matter carefully and made an investigation of the previous life of the candidates. As a usual procedure, soldiers were to be required to spend three years in probation before receiving the habit.[4] In a letter to Fortunatus, Bishop of Naples, the same Pope commanded that all who wished to be received into the monasteries of that region first had to undergo a two-year novitiate. The purpose of this period, he said, was to prove the character of the candidates and to give greater assurance that they were entering the religious life voluntarily. In the same letter he forbade the abbots of that region to receive soldiers into their monasteries until the previous consent of the Pope for their admission had been obtained.[5] This letter was later incorporated in the *Decretum Gratiani.*[6]

A letter from the Abbot Urbicus and the notary Hadrian elicited the same response from Gregory, to the effect that a married

[3] Can. 5—"Propterea ergo statuit sancta Synodus, ut nemo monastico habitu dignus putetur, prius quam triennii tempus ad experientiam eis relictum, eos esse probatos et tali esse vita dignos ostenderit: et haec omni modo observari praecepit, praeterquam si aliquis gravis morbus incidens probationis tempora contrahi coegerit, vel si nondum quis sit vir religiosus et tamen vitam monasticam in habitu saeculari peragat. Tali enim viro ad absolutam experientiam tempus semestre suffecerit."—Mansi, XVI, 539.

[4] *Ep. XI* —— ". . . et iuxta normam regularem debet in suo habitu per triennium probari, et tunc monachicum habitum Deo auctore suscipere."—Mansi, X, 92.

[5] *Ep. XXIII*—Mansi, X, 223.

[6] C. 6, C. XIX, q. 3.

person could not be received into the novitiate unless the spouse was also willing to enter religion.[7]

In a letter to Anthemius, Pope Gregory forbade him to receive any candidates into the monastery before they had reached eighteen years of age. This legislation was extended to all monasteries located on the islands of the Mediterranean,[8] and was incorporated in the Decretals of Gregory IX (1234).[9]

In settling the case of the priest Gonsaldus, Pope Alexander II (1061–1073) appealed to the Rule of Saint Benedict and the decrees of Pope Gregory the Great to support his response that a one-year probationary period was required for a valid monastic profession.[10]

In their comments on this text, the Glossators stated that there were other texts in Gratian which required a two- or three-year period for the novitiate, and remarked that these texts were incorporated for the sake of showing that the time period was arbitrary. They suggested that an unknown cleric and a known layman had to undergo a two-year novitiate, while a one-year period was sufficient for a known cleric.[11]

---

[7] *Ep. XLIX* (ad Urbicum Abbatem)—Mansi, X, 33; *Ep. XLIV* (ad Hadrianum Notarium)—Mansi, X, 285.

[8] *Ep. XLVIII*—Mansi, IX, 1068.

[9] C. 6, X, *de regularibus et transeuntibus in religionem,* III, 31; Jaffé, *Regesta Pontificum Romanorum ab condita Ecclesia ad annum post Christum natum MCXCVIII* (ed. 2 correctam et auctam auspiciis Guilelmi Wattenbach curaverunt S. Loewenfeld, F. Kaltenbrunner, P. Ewald, 2 vols. in 1, Lipsiae, 1885–1888), n. 1120 (hereafter cited Jaffé).

[10] C. 1, C. XVII, q. 2.

[11] *Glossa Ordinaria,* ad c. 1, C. XVII, q. 2, s. v. *unius anni.*

CHAPTER III

DECRETAL LEGISLATION

Pope Alexander III (1159–1181) stated that the novice was at complete liberty to leave the novitiate and return to the world, a point which was also clearly indicated in the Benedictine Rule.[1] Later Popes again affirmed this freedom, and took steps to see that no one was forced to embrace the religious life. Pope Innocent III (1198–1216), on May 15, 1204, in responding to a query, declared that a novice could return to the world.[2] Pope Gregory IX (1227–1241), on March 18, 1231, reaffirmed this right, provided that the novice had not made a private vow to enter and remain in the religious life.[3] The same decree provided that the habits of those about to be professed were to be blessed, so that they might be distinguished from the habits of the novices.

Innocent III, in a response to Ubaldus, Archbishop of Pisa, set forth the twofold purpose of the novitiate: to allow the monastery to observe the character of the candidate, and to allow the candidate to determine his suitability for the religious life. The Pontiff then noted that a practice existed in certain monasteries of that region to allow novices to be advanced to profession before they had completed the required period of probation. He decided that such persons were validly professed and were truly monks. But he strictly forbade any continuance of the practice in the future, and advised that abbots who presumed to advance novices to profession during the period of novitiate were to be corrected

[1] C. 9, X, *de regularibus et transeuntibus in religionem,* III, 31; Jaffé, n. 13946.

[2] C. 20, X, *de regularibus et transeuntibus in religionem,* III, 31; Potthast, *Regesta Pontificum Romanorum, inde ab anno post Christum natum MCXCVIII ad annum MCCCIV* (2 vols., Berolini, 1874–1875), n. 2209 (hereafter cited Potthast).

[3] C. 23, X, *de regularibus et transeuntibus in religionem,* III, 31; Potthast, n. 9650.

with a warning, for the probationary period was instituted "*in subsidium fragilitatis humanae.*" [4]

Perhaps the most important legislation regarding the novitiate that is found in the Decretals is the Decree of Pope Innocent IV (1243–1254). In a letter addressed to the Friars Preachers on June 17, 1244, he directed that the members of that Order complete a full year of probation, under penalty of the invalidity of their subsequent profession.[5] A letter of Pope Alexander IV (1254–1261), written in similar language, was addressed to both the Order of Friars Minor and the Order of Friars Preachers. In it the Pontiff forbade superiors in these Orders, by virtue of obedience and under penalty of excommunication, to admit aspirants to profession before they had completed the novitiate, or to restrict the liberty of the novices to transfer to another community or to return to the world. Friars professed in this manner would not be bound to the Order in any way; and the superiors who presumed to ignore the provisions of the letter were to be punished according to the Constitutions of their Order.[6]

The Rule of the Order of Friars Minor (founded in 1208) was given oral approval by Pope Innocent III in 1210. Again, in 1215, at the IV Lateran Council, the same Pope announced that he had approved the Franciscans and their Rule. However, since no written document of approval had emanated from the Council, it was left to his successor, Honorius III (1216–1227), to give formal written approval to the Order and the Rule. This he did in the Constitution "*Solet*" of November 29, 1223.[7] It provided for a one-year period of probation. Only the provincial superiors had the authority to admit candidates into the novitiate. This was a departure from previous Rules, in which such matters had been left to the discretion of the local superior or abbot of the monastery.

---

[4] C. 16, X, *de regularibus et transeuntibus in religionem,* III, 31; Potthast, n. 434.

[5] Mansi, XXIII, 565–566; Potthast, n. 11416.

[6] C. 2, *de regularibus et transeuntibus ad religionem,* III, 14, in VI°.

[7] *Bullarum Diplomatum et Privilegiorum Sanctorum Romanorum Pontificum Taurinensis Editio* (25 vols., Augustae Taurinorum, 1857–1872), III, 394 (hereafter cited *Bull. Rom. Taur.*).

Boniface VIII (1294–1303) extended the decrees of Pope Innocent IV and Pope Alexander IV, which had applied only to the Friars Preachers and Friars Minor, to all the Mendicant Orders.[8] The same Pope also extended the *privilegium canonis* to novices. In consequence of this decree, anyone who struck a novice became liable to excommunication.[9]

Finally, Pope Clement V (1305–1314) in the General Council of Vienne (1311–1312) directed that a novice master be appointed in all novitiates. His duties were to direct the novice along the path of perfection and to instruct him in the proper observance of religious discipline.[10]

---

[8] C. 3, *de regularibus et transeuntibus ad religionem,* III, 14, in VI°.

[9] C. 21, *de sententia excommunicationis, suspensionis et interdicti,* V, 11, in VI°.

[10] C. 1, *de statu monachorum vel canonicorum regularium,* III, 10, in Clem.

CHAPTER IV

LEGISLATION OF THE COUNCIL OF TRENT

1. *Establishment of the Year of Probation*

On November 20, 1563, the Fathers of the Council of Trent met to discuss the proposed schema of two decrees: one, *de reformatione regularium;* the other, *de reformatione monialium.* The former comprised twenty-three canons, the latter, seven. The proposed decrees touched many phases of regular discipline. The seventeenth canon of the proposed *Decretum de reformatione regularium* was concerned with legislation regarding the novitiate and profession.

> In quacumque religione professio non fiat ante 18 annum expletum. Durante vero novitiatu nulla eorum qui novitii sunt, valida sit obligatio, nec cum parentibus consanguineis ceterisve, nec renuntiatio bonorum cum juramento aliisve solemnitatibus, etiam in favorem piae causae, efficax sit, nec praedictae obligationes effectum sortiantur nisi post novitiatum, secuta solita votorum emissione, et omnes sub hac conditione factae censeantur etiamsi in obligationibus nulla ejus mentio habeatur. Nec huic constitutioni renuntiari ullo modo possit. Finito tempore novitiatus, superiores inducant novitios quos habiles invenerint, ad profitendum, aut e monasterio eos ejiciant. Per haec tamen sancta synodus non intendit aliquid innovare, aut prohibere, quin clerici Societatis Jesu, juxta eorum institutum, a Sancta Sede approbatum, professionem suam differre.[1]

During the discussion which followed the reading of the first draft of the two Decrees, the Fathers of the Council suggested that the two Decrees be united under the title *Decretum de regu-*

[1] *Concilii Tridentini Diariorum, Actorum, Epistularum, Tractatuum, Nova Collectio* (13 vols., Friburgi Brisgoviae: Herder & Co., 1901–1938), Vol. IX, *Pars Sexta Actorum* (collegit, illustravit, edidit Stephanus Ehses, 1924), p. 1038 (hereafter cited Ehses, *Collectio*).

laribus et monialibus, and this was done. The discussion of chapter 17 of the proposed *Decretum* showed many differences among the prelates. Some proposed that the age for religious profession be the same as that required for a valid marriage—14 years for males, 12 for females. Others felt that religious profession should be permitted at 15 or 16 years. A few suggested that the age be set at 20 years. Still others proposed that profession be made in the year in which the candidate was to receive the subdiaconate. Some of the Fathers asked for a two-year novitiate period, and others were of the opinion that each individual Rule should be observed in this matter.[2]

The age finally agreed upon was sixteen years, completed. Before the discussions were concluded, the Fathers divided the chapter into two, and restated the wording so that it became clearer and more emphatic. The *Decretum de regularibus et monialibus* was promulgated in the Twenty-fifth Session of the Council, on December 4, 1563. Chapters 15 and 16 dealt with the novitiate and religious profession.

> C. 15. In quacumque religione tam virorum quam mulierum professio non fiat ante decimum sextum annum expletum, nec qui minore tempore quam per annum post susceptum habitum in probatione steterit, ad professionem admittatur. Professio autem antea facta sit nulla, nullamque inducat obligationem ad alicujus regulae vel religionis vel ordinis observationem, aut ad alios quoscumque effectus.
> C. 16. Nulla quoque renunciatio aut obligatio antea facta, etiam cum juramento vel in favorem cujuscumque causae piae, valeat, nisi cum licentia episcopi sive ejus vicarii fiat intra duos menses proximos ante professionem, ac non alias intelligatur effectum sortiri, nisi secuta professione; aliter vero facta, etiamsi cum hujus favoris expressa renunciatione, etiam jurata, sit irrita et nullius effectus. Finito vero tempore novitiatus superiores novitios, quos habiles invenerint, ad profitendum admittant, aut e monasterio eos ejiciant. Per haec tamen sancta synodus non intendit aliquid innovare aut prohibere, quin religio clericorum Societatis Jesu juxta pium eorum institutum a sancta Sede Apostolica approbatum Domino

[2] Ehses, *Collectio,* pp. 1036–1085.

> et ejus ecclesiae inservire possit. Sed neque ante professionem, excepto victo et vestitu novitii vel novitiae illius temporis, quo in probatione est, quocumque praetextu a parentibus vel propinquis aut curatoribus ejus monasterio aliquid ex bonis ejusdem tribuatur, ne hac occasione discedere nequeat, quod totam vel majorem partem substantiae suae monasterium possideat, nec facile, si discesserit, id recuperare possit. Quin potius praecipit sub anathematis poena dantibus et recipientibus, ne hoc ullo modo fiat, et ut abeuntibus ante professionem omnia restituantur, quae sua erant. Quod ut recte fiat, episcopus etiam censuras ecclesiasticas, si opus fuerit, compellat.[3]

It should be noted that the legislation of the Council of Trent was applicable only to those communities whose members took the three solemn vows of religion. The decree referred to solemn profession and its validity, and hence communities with simple vows were not bound by the legislation. For simple vows, the will of the one making the vow was sufficient. Hence, in such congregations simple vows were valid even if profession had been preceded by a shorter probationary period or by none at all.[4] Nevertheless it was the constant practice of the Sacred Congregations to apply this legislation even to congregations whose members took simple vows,[5] a practice eventually canonized by the Code of Canon Law.[6]

The earlier provision of the old law, which allowed the aspirant to be validly professed if the religious community waived the requirement of all or part of the probationary period,[7] was abrogated by the Council of Trent. Commentators stated that the *Decretum de regularibus et monialibus* implicitly declared that the

---

[3] Schroeder, *Canons and Decrees of the Council of Trent, Text, Translation and Commentary* (St. Louis-London: B. Herder & Co., 1941), pp. 494–495.

[4] Bouix, *Tractatus de Jure Regularium* (2 vols., Parisiis, 1857), I, 577–578.

[5] Wernz, *Ius Decretalium ad Usum Praelectionum in Scholis Textus Canonici sive Iuris Decretalium* (2. ed., 6 vols., Romae et Prati, 1906–1913), III, n. 644 (hereafter cited *Ius Decretalium*).

[6] Can. 572.

[7] C. 16, X, *de regularibus et transeuntibus in religionem,* III, 31.

one-year probation period was of the very form and substance of the novitiate. In addition, since the novitiate was established for the purpose of giving the novice an opportunity to test the religious life and of allowing the religious community to observe the qualities of the aspirant, it was of its very nature closely related to the common good, from which private agreements could not derogate.[8]

The Sacred Congregation of the Council expressly declared that the probationary period could not be renounced by either the aspirant or the religious Order, and that profession made without it was null and void.[9] Fagnanus (1598–1678) related that the same Sacred Congregation gave a response which stated that the period of probation could not be waived, even when the candidate had made a vow to enter religion.[10]

Although the Council of Trent established the age of sixteen years completed as an essential condition for the validity of religious profession, no mention was made of the valid age for the beginning of the novitiate and the reception of the habit. It seems that it was the intention of the Fathers to establish the age of fifteen years completed as the minimum age for entering the novitiate. The reason for this assumption is that the Council provided that at the conclusion of the year's probation the novices who were judged suitable should be admitted to profession, and that those who were unsuitable should be dismissed. The implication seemed to be that profession was to follow immediately upon the conclusion of the novitiate.[11]

---

[8] Schmalzgrueber, *Ius Ecclesiasticum Universum* (5 vols. in 12, Romae, 1843–1845), Lib. IV, tit. XXXI, n. 46 (hereafter cited *Ius Ecclesiasticum*); Reiffenstuel, *Ius Canonicum Universum* (5 vols., Parisiis, 1864–1870), Lib. III, tit. XXXI, n. 92 (hereafter cited *Ius Canonicum*).

[9] Pallottini, *Collectio omnium conclusionum et resolutionum quae in causis propositis apud Sacram Congregationem Cardinalium S. Concilii Tridentini Interpretum prodierunt ab eius institutione, anno MDLXXIX ad MDCCCLX, distinctis titulis alphabetico ordine per materias digesta* (18 vols., Romae, 1868–1895), Vol. XV, s. v. *Professio religiosa,* II, n. 18 (hereafter cited Pallottini).

[10] *Commentarium in Quinque Libros Decretalium* (4 vols., Venetiis, 1697), Lib. III, c. XX, n. 42 (hereafter cited *Commentarium*).

[11] Sess. XXV, *de regularibus,* c. 16.

Schmalzgrueber (1663–1735), however, disagreed with this conclusion. He was of the opinion that the previous law regarding the reception into the novitiate had been left unchanged. The Tridentine Law, he stated, was not given absolutely, but with the hypothetical condition, *nisi aliquid obstet*. One who had completed his sixteenth year only after he had fulfilled the full period of probation could not be professed immediately at the conclusion of the novitiate, but had to wait until he had reached the required age, for the reason that he was impeded from profession by the obstacle occasioned through the lack of age. Therefore, Schmalzgrueber concluded, the novitiate could be entered at an age even earlier than fifteen years.[12] Fagnanus stated that the Sacred Congregation of the Council inclined to the opinion that the Council of Trent did not intend to set any definite age for the valid reception of the religious habit.[13]

2. *Continuity of the Novitiate Year*

The Decree of the Council of Trent which required a full year's novitiate before profession was an extension of the Decree *Non solum* of Innocent IV.[14] The Decree of the eminent Pontiff was interpreted by commentators most strictly, and the same rigorous interpretation was applied to the Tridentine legislation. The novitiate year was to be continuous, uninterrupted, and computed from the actual moment when it began.

Practically all the commentators were in agreement that the novitiate year should be continuous and uninterrupted. Reiffenstuel (1642–1703) pointed out that the purpose of the novitiate was to subject the candidate to the rigors and hardships of the religious life, and that this postulated a complete year of trial. The novitiate would fail to achieve its purpose if the year were broken up into small periods of time, and the novice would not be fully or fairly subjected to the Rule and its practice.[15] Schmalzgrueber noted that when the law required a definite time period which was to be computed from one day to another, it was to be

[12] *Ius Ecclesiasticum,* Lib. IV, tit. XXXI, n. 44.

[13] *Commentarium,* Lib. III, c. XVI, n. 14.

[14] C. 2, *de regularibus et transeuntibus ad religionem,* III, 14, in VI°.

[15] *Ius Canonicum,* Lib. III, tit. XXXI, n. 104.

understood as meaning an uninterrupted period, unless the subject matter of the law or the will of the lawgiver implied a contrary interpretation.[16] The Sacred Congregation of the Council consistently held that religious profession was invalid unless a complete, continuous and uninterrupted probationary year had preceded the act of profession.[17]

It was held, moreover, that the novitiate was to be computed from the very moment it began, and that a complete year had to elapse between the time of investiture in the habit (or entrance into the novitiate) and the time of profession. It was asserted that it was in no way permitted to anticipate profession, by even the shortest period of time, under penalty of the invalidity of the profession.[18] The Sacred Congregation of the Council ruled, in 1617, that profession made after a novitiate which was incomplete by only two hours was invalid.[19]

Fagnanus related that the profession in similar cases which were brought to the same Sacred Congregation for a decision were declared invalid. No public declaration was made, however, lest scruples and anxieties arise in religious communities.[20]

3. *Rights and Privileges of Novices*

Traditionally the novices in any religious community enjoyed certain definite rights and privileges. Foremost among these was the right freely to leave the novitiate and to return to the world. The novitiate was a period of trial and preparation, and the novice was not burdened with any obligations in justice to the community. If he perceived that he was not adapted to the religious life, he was always at complete liberty to depart.[21]

Moreover, he had the right not to be dismissed without a just cause. If he felt that he had been aggrieved in this matter, he

---

[16] *Ius Ecclesiasticum,* Lib. IV, tit. XXXI, n. 68.

[17] Pallottini, Vol. XV, s. v. *Professio religiosa,* II, nn. 7, 8, 10, 11, 25, 26.

[18] *Synopsis Pirhingiana seu SS. Canonum Doctrina ex fusioribus quinque libris Henrici Pirhing in Compendium Redacta* (Romae, 1849), p. 516 (hereafter cited *Synopsis Pirhingiana*).

[19] *Pallottini,* Vol. XV, s. v. *Professio religiosa,* II, n. 4.

[20] *Commentarium,* Lib. III, c. XVI, n. 23.

[21] Cc. 9, 20, 23, X, *de regularibus et transeuntibus in religionem,* III, 31.

was accorded a right to seek redress with the superior, who, upon proof of an unjust dismissal, was required to effect a *restitutio in integrum* and to readmit him to the novitiate.[22] Every novice who had been legitimately received into the novitiate was acknowledged as possessing a *ius ad rem* relative to religious profession, a right regarding which it was held he could not be deprived without a just cause. A notable injury was done to anyone who was without a justifying reason dismissed from a novitiate, inasmuch as he thereby suffered to some extent a loss of good name and reputation. When the dismissal was effected without a good reason, unjust injury was done, and hence by way of remedy a redress could always be sought.[23]

The commentators taught further that a religious superior who denied profession to a worthy and properly qualified candidate involved himself in grave sin, and that he likewise incurred the guilt of sin if he admitted an unworthy novice to profession. In the first case, they maintained, unjust injury was committed against the novice; in the latter case, they contended, the injury was done to the public welfare of the Church and the religious community.

Novices, so it was held, enjoyed all the privileges of the religious community which they entered.[24] Although they were not properly called religious, they nevertheless formed part of a specially privileged community, and it was consistently argued that they could not be deprived, without a just cause, of the favors and privileges which were enjoyed by the community as a whole. "*Qui sentit onus, sentire debet commodum, et e contra.*" [25]

In consequence it was held that they enjoyed the *privilegium canonis,* immunity from trial in the civil courts, and all the indulgences and spiritual favors which had been granted to the professed religious of their community.[26]

The legislation of the Council of Trent forbade, in a most strict

[22] Pignatelli, *Consultationes Canonicae* (11 toms. in 4 vols., Coloniae Allobrogum, 1790), Tom. IV, cons. 201, n. 3.

[23] Reiffenstuel, *Ius Canonicum,* Lib. III, tit. XXXI, n. 114.

[24] Pignatelli, *Consultationes Canonicae,* Tom. IV, cons. 119, n. 7; *Synopsis Pirhingiana,* p. 519.

[25] Reg. 55, R. J., in VI°.

[26] Fagnanus, *Commentarium,* Lib. III, c. XXIII, n. 45; "*odia restringi, et favores convenit ampliari.*"—Reg. 15, R. J., in VI°.

manner, the acceptance of any money or other goods from the novice himself, his parents, relatives or guardians, except a moderate sum which was to be used for the food and clothing of the novice.[27] The Fathers of the Council were most desirous to preserve the complete liberty of the novice to leave the novitiate, if he felt that he was not suited to the religious life. They realized that this much desired liberty would be impaired if the aspirant's means of sustenance were taken away, either in whole or in part, while he was in the novitiate. A further motive which impelled the enactment of this legislation was to give religious superiors complete freedom in admitting or rejecting candidates for profession, lest any profession be tainted with the crime of simony.[28] The Tridentine legislation was an amplification and extension of the earlier Decretal legislation of Boniface VIII.[29]

[27] Sess. XXV, *de regularibus*, c. 16.

[28] Fagnanus, *Commentarium*, Lib. III, c. XXIII, n. 49.

[29] C. 4, *de regularibus et transeuntibus ad religionem*, III, 14, in VI°.

CHAPTER V

LATER PAPAL LEGISLATION

Within a few decades after the Council of Trent, several of the Popes enacted legislation bearing upon the novitiate and the reception of candidates. One of the most important of these was the Constitution of Sixtus V (1585–1590), *Cum de omnibus,* of November 26, 1587.[1] In it the Pontiff decreed that children born of an incestuous or sacrilegious marriage were not to be received into the novitiate or to religious profession, under penalty of the invalidity of the reception and profession. Other children born out of lawful wedlock, even though legitimated by the subsequent marriage of their parents, were not to be received until a thorough investigation of their habits and their character had been made, and then only with the unanimous consent of the Provincial or General Chapter. Further, lest anyone suspected of a grave crime or burdened with a heavy debt should seek to enter the religious life as an escape from possible punishment by the civil authority, the Pontiff provided that all candidates for admission had to be thoroughly investigated, and that they were to be admitted only by the Provincial or the General Superior with the consent of their respective counsellors. Receptions made contrary to the provisions of the Constitution were completely lacking in canonical effect.

Evidently, serious doubts arose concerning the interpretation of the Constitution, for less than a year later, on October 21, 1588, the same Pope issued another Constitution, *Ad Romanum.*[2] This later document was more specific in its provisions, and attempted to eliminate any difficulties in the interpretation and implementation of the Constitution *Cum de omnibus.* Persons of illegitimate

[1] *Codicis Iuris Canonici Fontes,* cura Emi Petri Card. Gasparri editi (9 vols., Romae [postea Civitate Vaticana]: Typis Polyglottis Vaticanis, 1923–1939. [Vols. VII–IX, ed. cura et studio Emi Iustiniani Card. Serédi], n. 162 (hereafter cited *Fontes*).

[2] *Fontes,* n. 164.

birth who had entered the religious life without papal dispensation and before the publication of the Constitution *Cum de omnibus,* and had since risen to offices of honor and dignity in their communities, were to be removed from office and deprived of the dignity which they enjoyed.

Some of the prescriptions of the legislation of Sixtus V proved incapable of execution and worked a severe hardship on some religious who had risen to offices of honor in their communities. Accordingly, on March 15, 1591, Gregory XIV (1590–1591) published the Constitution *Circumspecta,* in which he ordered that all religious who had been deprived of their office by the Sixtine legislation should be restored to the office which they had held prior to the publication of the Constitution *Cum de omnibus.*[3] The investigation of the manner of life and of the character of the candidates for reception was to be carefully carried out. In monasteries which had an autonomous status (*sui iuris*), the admission of candidates was reserved to the superior of the monastery and his counsellors.

Clement VIII (1592–1605), seeking to restore religious discipline, ordered, in three separate documents, that no one was to receive the religious habit except in houses which were designated by the papal authority.[4] Superiors who violated the provisions of these decrees were *ipso facto* deprived of their office and of the right to vote in their community, and were declared incapable of holding any office in their Order or congregation. The reception of novices in any house other than that designated by the Holy See was to be null and void of all juridic effect.

In his Constitution *Cum ad regularem* of March 19, 1603, Pope Clement VIII enacted specific rules for the reception of novices and the administration of the novitiate.[5] In summary, the following were the provisions of this legislation: No one was to be received into the novitiate until he had reached the age prescribed by the Constitutions of the Order or congregation. Per-

---

[3] *Fontes,* n. 170.

[4] Const. *Regularis disciplinae,* 12 mart. 1596—*Fontes,* n. 183; Const. *Cum iamdudum,* 20 iun. 1599—*Bull. Rom. Taur.,* X, 770; Const. *Qui alias,* 19 maii 1602—*Bull. Rom. Taur.,* X, 771–772.

[5] *Fontes,* n. 189.

sons without the proper educational requirements were to be admitted as candidates for the lay brotherhood only. Superiors were to inquire into the reasons for the aspirant's decision to enter the religious life. Novices were to be thoroughly instructed regarding the religious life, as also regarding the special customs and practices of the Order or congregation, and of its constitutions.

As soon as they were received into the novitiate, the novices were to make a general confession of their entire past life. The novitiate itself was to be separated from that part of the house in which the professed members lived. Professed members were not to enter the precincts of the novitiate without the permission of the superior and the novice master. The novice master was to be chosen by the provincial chapter for a three-year period; he was to be a priest, at least thirty-five years of age, and professed at least ten years. If there was need, he could be given an associate (*socius*), who was to be a priest at least thirty years old.

Both the novice master and his associate were to be free from any office or duty which would impede them in the care and government of the novices. They were to be men who were outstanding for their practice of mortification, for their prudence, for their charity and their zeal. To the novice master alone belonged the right and the duty of training the novices, and he alone was responsible for the government of the novitiate. No one could interfere in these matters except the superior general and the visitator.

Every novice was required to give some time to mental prayer twice daily, to attend Holy Mass and to make an examination of conscience every day. Toward the end of the probationary period the novices were to submit to another examination. If they were found to be suitable candidates for the religious life, they were to be admitted to profession.

Superiors and others who violated any of the provisions of this legislation were subject to deprivation of office and even greater penalties.

This Constitution of Clement VIII was one of the most important documents touching on the subject of the training of novices. Its wise provisions have become incorporated almost verbatim in the Code of Canon Law.

CHAPTER VI

THE ESTABLISHMENT OF QUASI-RELIGIOUS SOCIETIES

One of the sure marks of the vitality of the Church has been its ability to adapt itself to changing conditions. Though the truths of our faith have always remained the same, though the body of Catholic doctrine has never changed, the long centuries of the Church's history have provided it with a certain resiliency which has enabled it to cope with the many perplexing problems that arose. This has been particularly true in the history of the religious life.

In the early centuries of the Church, men and women banded together to form monastic communities. "*Orare et laborare*" was the watchword of the early monks and cenobites. They passed their days in prayer, meditation and manual labor. Later ages saw the rise of the Mendicant Orders, whose Rules combined both the active and the contemplative life. These were followed by religious communities which had a specialized work. Some were founded with a view to assisting in the redemption of captives; others, with the aim of caring for the sick and of administering hospitals; others, with the purpose of devoting themselves to education; and still others, for the sake of preaching missions and of animating the faith of the people.

The centuries since the Council of Trent witnessed the establishment of communities whose members did not take the customary public vows of religion, but were bound only by private vows, by an oath, by a promise, or by no strictly juridic bond whatsoever. The members followed, to some extent, the religious mode of life. The absence of the three public vows, however, gave these communities a certain flexibility, and enabled them to engage in works which ordinarily were not performed by the religious communities. The projected work of some of these "quasi-religious" communities was to conduct seminaries and to educate young men for the priesthood; of others, to engage largely in missionary activities; of still others, to undertake the preaching of missions and the performance of other apostolic works. The Holy See always looked favorably upon this type of organization, and granted many favors and privileges to the individual communities.

The legislation which governed societies without vows was largely particular rather than common law, and its details had to be ascertained from the constitutions of the various societies. However, the Code of Canon Law, promulgated in 1917, devotes an entire title to norms provided for them.[1]

1. *The Brethren of the Common Life*

The Brethren of the Common Life were founded in Holland by Geert de Groote (1340–1384). A canon of the Cathedral of Utrecht, he resigned his benefice in 1373 and lived in solitude for seven years. Then, feeling himself constrained to go forth and preach, he went from place to place calling men to repentance and bewailing the relaxation of ecclesiastical discipline and the degradation of the clergy. A little band of followers attached themselves to Groote, became his co-workers, and formed the "Brethren of the Common Life." Many of the secular clergy enrolled themselves in his Brotherhood, which was in due course approved by the Holy See.

The Brethren of the Common Life resembled in some respects the Beghard and Beguine communities which had flourished two centuries earlier and were then decadent. The members took no vows, neither asked nor received alms; their first aim was to cultivate the interior life, and they worked for their daily bread. Their houses were closely knit together. The lay members occupied themselves with literature and education, and the priests with preaching. Their schools became centers of spiritual and intellectual life. Before the close of the fifteenth century, Germany and the Netherlands were studded with schools conducted by the Brethren. Many of these institutions were swept away in the religious troubles of the sixteenth century. Others languished

[1] Lib. II, tit. XVII, cans. 673–681.

until the French Revolution, while the rise of universities, the creation of diocesan seminaries and the competition of new teaching Orders gradually extinguished both the schools and the Brotherhood.[2]

2. *The Oratorians of St. Philip Neri*

The Congregation of the Oratory owed its foundation to St. Philip Neri (1515–1595). Ordained to the priesthood in 1551, he busied himself with priestly labors in the city of Rome. Several of the Roman clergy joined him in his work and asked to be taken under his spiritual direction. In 1564 the little group decided to form itself into a community, which was given charge of the church of Santa Maria in Vallicella. There they occupied themselves in preaching, meditation and the conducting of religious devotions for the laity. On July 15, 1575, Pope Gregory XIII (1572–1585) gave his approval to the new congregation in the Bull *Copiosus.*[3] Thus a new religious family was born into the Church—a congregation of secular priests without vows, leading a community life—a congregation which the religious exigencies of the times made necessary, a type of life unknown in the Middle Ages.[4]

At the beginning the Oratorians had no constitutions or Rule, but relied upon the example and advice of their founder. However, towards the end of the sixteenth century, a written constitution was drawn up. This constitution was approved and confirmed by Pope Paul V (1605–1621) in the Bull *Christifidelium* of February 24, 1612.[5]

The members of the Congregation were not bound together by any bond other than that of charity, and were free to leave the Institute whenever they so desired. The constitutions provided that if the community decided at any time to bind the members by vows, oath or promise, all the goods of the community were to revert to the members who remained true to the ideal of St. Philip and remained as secular priests without vows. This was to be

[2] *The Catholic Encyclopedia,* s. v. *Common Life, Brethren of,* IV, 166.
[3] *Bull. Rom. Taur.,* VIII, 541.
[4] André George, *L'Oratoire* (Paris: Bernard Grasset, 1928), p. 17.
[5] *Bull. Rom. Taur.,* XII, 37–57.

observed even if an overwhelming majority of the members supported any attempt to bind themselves by any bond other than that of charity. Each house was to be autonomous. "*Unaquaeque domus aut familia nostrae formam imitata, separatim ab aliis per se regatur et moderetur.*"[6]

3. *The Oblates of St. Ambrose*

In 1578 the saintly Cardinal Charles Borromeo (1538–1584), Archbishop of Milan (1565–1584), wrote:

> . . . I have finally decided to commence, with God's help, the work I have so long meditated, namely, the founding of an Order of clerics who are already priests, under the title of the Oblates of St. Ambrose. They will live in community, following the rules that I or my successors will lay down for their guidance. They will not be allowed to accept a benefice outside their diocese. Their principal object will be to devote their lives to the service of the Ambrosian Rite, and after a sufficient probation they will make a vow to do so. They will preach, hear confessions, and administer the Sacraments wherever they are sent. They will direct schools, colleges and pious confraternities. In brief, they will do their utmost to promote the greater glory of God. . . .[7]

After the V Provincial Council of Milan (1579), Saint Charles Borromeo chose several diocesan priests whom he knew to be inclined to this manner of life. Their ranks were augmented by several others who had been touched by a discourse on this subject as given by the Cardinal at the Council. The Congregation was given the title "Oblates of the Blessed Virgin Mary and Saint Ambrose," and began its existence on August 16, 1579, with the approval of Pope Gregory XIII. In 1581 the statutes or "*Institutiones*" of the Congregation, which had been composed by the Cardinal himself, were issued. The members made a simple vow of obedience to the Archbishop of Milan. They vowed to recognize him as their superior, and to be united to him as members to

---

[6] *Bull. Rom. Taur.*, XII, 40–41.

[7] Stacpoole-Kenny, *Saint Charles Borromeo* (New York: Benziger Brothers, 1911), p. 168.

their leader; to will nothing but what he willed; to seek nothing but the glory of God and the good of souls; to have no other occupation but to assist the Archbishop in the conduct and government of the diocese; to accept any office which might be assigned to them.[8] The statutes and Rule of the community were approved by Pope Clement VIII in the Bull *Cum sicut accepimus* of December 5, 1600.

4. *The Oratorians of France*

The Oratory of Jesus or the French Oratory, as it is more commonly called, was founded by Pierre de Berulle (1575–1629) in 1611. Its purpose was to honor the mysteries of the Infancy, the Life and the Death of Jesus Christ and of His Holy Mother, and to strive to realize the fullest perfection of the priestly ideal. Its members were to occupy themselves in the education of clerics, in the administration of colleges, and in the preaching of the word of God to the people.[9] The Oratory expanded very rapidly, and on May 10, 1616, Pope Paul V gave papal approval to the new congregation in the Bull *Sacrosanctae Romanae Ecclesiae.*[10] The approval was confirmed by Innocent X (1644–1655) in the Brief *Ex Romani.*[11] Innocent's successor, Alexander VII (1655–1667), granted certain spiritual favors and privileges to the French Oratorians.[12]

The internal organization of the Oratory of Jesus was very much like that of the Roman Oratory. The members were united only by the bond of charity, and were free to leave at any time. However, the organization was centralized. The houses were not independent, but were governed by the authority of an elected superior general and his assistants.

During the seventeenth century the Oratory was torn by internal dissension, and with the coming of the French Revolution it

---

[8] Migne, *Encyclopedie Théologique* (3 series, 168 vols., Parisiis, 1845–1855), 1st series, *Dictionnaire des Ordres Réligieux,* XXII, 18–21.

[9] Hermant, *Histoire de l'Établissement des Ordres Réligieux et des Congrégations Régulières de l'Église* (Rouen, 1697), p. 401.

[10] *Bull. Rom. Taur.,* XII, 205–210.

[11] 19 nov. 1654—*Bull. Rom. Taur.,* XV, 777–779.

[12] Breve *Exponi nobis,* 12 sept. 1655—*Bull. Rom. Taur.,* XVI, 63–65.

passed out of existence. In 1852, however, the Congregation was reorganized under the leadership and inspiration of Fathers Gratry (1805–1872) and Petetot (1801–1887), and was approved by the Sacred Congregation of Bishops and Regulars on March 22, 1864.[13]

5. *The Congregation of the Mission*

The Congregation of the Mission was founded by St. Vincent de Paul (1581–1660) in 1625. For several years before, a group of priests had assisted him in the work of preaching missions. They had followed certain rules imposed by themselves, and then decided to establish themselves as a religious institute. Seven years later, on January 12, 1633, Pope Urban VIII (1623–1644) gave approval to the community in the Bull *Salvatoris nostri.* The authorization was subject to several restrictions. It was at first agreed that the Priests of the Mission were, and would remain, secular priests subject to the bishops and not professed with any religious vows. In place of the latter there was a promise of stability, an engagement of a purely natural order, which was not sanctioned by the spiritual power. But the holy founder understood the necessity of preserving his disciples from the temptation to inconstancy, and accordingly required all who wished to enter the Congregation to make, after a certain period of trial, four simple vows, substantially identical with those of religious.[14]

There was some resistance among the members, but after many discussions and an experience that lasted nearly thirty years the vows were accepted, but with this difference: the vows were to be private in nature, pronounced, not in the hands of the superior, but before and to the Blessed Sacrament, in the presence of the superior as witness and as a guarantee for the obligations assumed by the Congregation towards the new member.[15] The plan was

---

[13] *Analecta Iuris Pontificii* (Romae, 1855–1869; Parisiis, 1872–1891), VII (1864), 758 (hereafter cited *Analecta*).

[14] Pierre Coste, *Monsieur Vincent* (3 vols., Paris: Desclée, de Brouwer, 1931), II, 22.

[15] Pisani, *The Congregations of Priests from the Sixteenth to the Eighteenth Century* (translated by Mother Mary Reginald), (St. Louis: B. Herder & Co., 1930), pp. 76–77.

approved by Pope Alexander VII in the Bull *Ex commissa nobis* of September 22, 1655.[16] A two-year period of probation was necessary before the aspirant could be admitted to vows.

6. *The Secular Clerics of the Common Life*

The Secular Clerics of the Common Life were founded in 1643 by Bartholomew Holzhauser (1613–1658), a priest of the diocese of Mainz, in Germany. His purpose was to form a congregation of secular priests who would lead an apostolic life in community and become models of priestly perfection and zealous leaders of the people. Those who excelled in knowledge and virtue were to be placed as teachers in seminaries, to educate a new generation of priests willing to use all their talents and energy for the honor of God and the salvation of souls. The priests thus educated he would induce to join the community. The members were expected to live in the seminaries, or in groups of two and three in parishes, and to follow a set schedule of daily prayers and exercises. Funds were to be held in common. No vows were to be taken, but a simple promise of obedience made to the superior was to be confirmed with an oath.

The Secular Clerics had a rather unusual nature. They appeared to have the nature of a confraternity, rather than that of a religious or quasi-religious institute. The first paragraph of the constitutions, approved by Innocent XI (1676–1689) in 1680, stated: "Finis hujus vitae clericalis non est novum institutum aut religionem introducere, sed ipsummet statum clericalem et ecclesiasticum, a Christo fundatum et ab Apostolis observatum, sub immediata RR. Ordinariorum potestate, vere amplecti." [17]

Additions to the constitutions, approved by Innocent XI in 1684,[18] allowed three kinds of houses in each province: one for the education of clerics, another which was to serve as a place of residence for those who were engaged in the ministry, and a third for those who were incapacitated for work because of superannuation or illness. For each of these classes there were special

---

[16] *Bull. Rom. Taur.*, XVI, 67–69.

[17] *Bull. Rom. Taur.*, XIX, 242.

[18] Const. *Sacrosancti*, 17 apr. 1684—*Bull. Rom. Taur.*, XIX, 530–581.

rules. About the end of the seventeenth century the community began to decline and gradually disappeared.[19]

7. *The Congregation of Jesus and Mary*

The Congregation of Jesus and Mary was founded by Saint John Eudes (1601–1680) in 1643. He entered the French Oratory in 1623. After his ordination in 1625 he was employed for eleven years in the preaching of missions. He saw with grief that his community was withdrawing from the direction of seminaries and taking up the easier work of maintaining colleges. He therefore left the Oratory and established a separate community, under the patronage of Jesus and Mary, whose principal work was to be the education of clerics and the administration of seminaries. Following the example of the Oratory, the Eudists made a simple promise or "*engagement*" of stability and obedience.

St. John Eudes wrote the constitutions of the Congregation about 1652. He tried in vain to obtain papal approval for his community. His lack of success in this seemed to derive from the opposition of the French Oratorians. Molitor (1867–1926) stated that approval of the Holy See was given by Clement X in 1674,[20] but it seems that he confused the Congregation of Jesus and Mary with a lay confraternity of the same name, which received papal approval on October 4 of that year.[21]

However, the new community won the loyal support of many bishops, and the Roman authorities did give approval to the seminaries conducted by the members of the Congregation. At the death of the founder in 1680 the Congregation was solidly established. One hundred years later, on the eve of the French Revolution, it numbered several hundred priests, in charge of most of the seminaries in Normandy and Brittany.[22] The troubles of the Revolution dispersed the community and it was not re-established until 1826. The Congregation was approved by the

[19] Currier, *History of Religious Orders* (New York, 1896), p. 623.

[20] *Religiosi Juris Capita Selecta* (Ratisbon: Fr. Pustet, 1909), p. 65.

[21] A reproduction of the Decree of approval is found in Emile Georges' *Saint Jean Eudes* (Paris: Letheilleux, 1936), p. 264.

[22] Georges, *Saint Jean Eudes*, p. 462.

Sacred Congregation of Bishops and Regulars on April 3, 1857,[23] and the constitutions on August 13, 1874.

8. *Later Congregations without Vows*

Later centuries saw the rise of additional communities whose members did not take the usual public vows of religion. The Society of Saint Sulpice was founded by Jean Jacques Olier (1608–1657) in 1642. Its members made a simple promise, which could be annulled at the will of the subject as well as by the superiors. Each member retained his own property, but could not dispose of it without the consent of his superior.

The Society of the Catholic Apostolate (known until 1947 as the Pious Society of Missions) was founded by the Blessed Vincent Pallotti (1795–1850) in 1820. Its end is to revive faith and charity among Catholics, and to bring infidel and heretic nations to the faith of Christ.

The Congregation of the Most Precious Blood, founded by Blessed Gaspar del Bufalo (1786–1837), was approved by the Sacred Congregation of Bishops and Regulars on August 27, 1841.[24]

The Paulist Fathers were organized by Father Isaac Hecker (1819–1888) in 1858 to work for the conversion of America. The Mill Hill Fathers, established by Herbert Cardinal Vaughan (1832–1903) in 1866, labor in the foreign missions. The Society of Saint Joseph of the Sacred Heart, an offshoot of the Mill Hill Fathers, was established in 1893, and its members work among the Negroes in the United States. The White Fathers were organized by the eminent Cardinal Lavigerie (1825–1892) in 1867 to work for the conversion of Africa. The Catholic Foreign Mission Society of America (Maryknoll) was founded in 1911 as an American society of priests and brothers for the foreign missions.

---

[23] "Traité des Congrégations Séculiers," *Analecta*, V (1861), 90.

[24] "Traité des Congrégations Séculiers," *Analecta*, V (1861), 90.

CHAPTER VII

THE PROBATION IN THE EARLY CONSTITUTIONS OF SOCIETIES WITHOUT VOWS

1. *The Oratorians of St. Philip Neri*

The provisions for the probation in the Congregation of the Oratory were found in Chapter VI of the Constitutions.[1]

The Constitutions stated, first of all, that persons who aspired to membership in the Oratory had to be men of excellent character and proved virtue, "*maxime idonei et quasi ad institutum nati.*" They had to be at least eighteen years of age and no older than forty-five, not burdened with any canonical impediment which forbade the reception of Holy Orders, unless they intended to remain as lay members of the community. Admission was forbidden to those who were in ill health, who had previously entered some religious community, or whose reputation was questionable. It was preferable that candidates be those who had frequently attended the exercises and devotions at the Oratory, who had some knowledge of the aims and purposes of the Congregation, and who had one of the Fathers of the Oratory as their regular confessor. Aspirants could, however, be dispensed from any of these prerequisites, provided that this met with the approval of the older Fathers.

Before his admission, two of the Fathers of the Congregation were chosen to make diligent inquiry concerning the qualifications of the candidate. They were to hold frequent conferences with him, and were permitted to question his relatives and acquaintances. Upon completing their investigation they were to make a report to the entire community. The other Fathers were also to inquire into the motives of the aspirant, and they also were directed to make a report to the community.

Then the provost was to invite the candidate to live in the house for a few days, at the conclusion of which he was, by secret vote

[1] *Bull. Rom. Taur.*, XII, 44–45.

of the decennial Fathers (those in the community for ten years or more), either admitted or dismissed. When admitted he was to live for one month as a guest, in order that he might observe the manner of life in the Oratory and make his choice a matter of more mature deliberation. If, upon the conclusion of this one month's residence, he was admitted to the probation of the first year by the provost and his deputies, he was entrusted to the care of the prefect of novices, who was to be one of the most mature and obedient members of the community. The candidate's name was then inscribed in the book set aside for this purpose, and the year of first probation began.

If the novice had given indications of an Oratorian vocation, then at the conclusion of the first year the provost and his deputies were to admit him to the second probationary period, which lasted for two years; otherwise, he was to be dismissed. During the entire three-year period of probation the prefect of novices was to be engaged in helping the novices, by every possible means, to advance in virtue. He was to see that they served Holy Mass daily, even if the novices were priests themselves; that they abstained from studies, according to the discretion of the superior; that they served at table; that they read at church and were present at the sermons; that they followed the community exercises; that they acted as porter; that they did not leave the house alone, or without permission; that they did not occupy themselves with external affairs; that they cared for the sacristy and decorated the altars; that they went to confession three times weekly and received Holy Communion at the discretion of their confessor; and that they approached the prefect twice monthly for a conference on spiritual matters.

At the conclusion of the three years of probation the novice was, if judged suitable, admitted to the Congregation by the secret vote of all the Fathers who had been in the community for ten years or more. His name was inscribed in the Book of Admissions and he was considered an Oratorian from that time onward.

2. *The Oblates of St. Ambrose*

Chapter XVII of the Constitutions of the Oblates of St. Ambrose set forth the provisions for the admission of candidates into the Congregation.[2] The right of admitting members belonged only to the Archbishop. Admission was to be denied to persons who had left or who had been dismissed from any religious congregation, unless it was evident that they had departed for a just and reasonable cause.

The aspirant first presented a petition for admission to the Archbishop, who subjected the candidate to an examination of his intention and his reasons for desiring to join the Oblates. This investigation concluded, the candidate was assigned to the spiritual prefect or some other prudent priest of the community, who was to instruct him concerning the nature, the purpose and the customs of the Oblates. The spiritual prefect was also instructed to make inquiry concerning the qualifications of the aspirant, to determine his intentions, and to learn if there was any obstacle which might impede his reception. At the conclusion of this investigation the prefect submitted a report to the provost, together with his opinion as to the advisability of accepting the candidate. The provost, in turn, submitted this report to the entire community, whose members expressed their opinions on the matter. The provost then turned over their report to the Archbishop, and the latter made the final decision either to accept or to reject the candidate.

The applicant was sent to the motherhouse of the Oblates to undergo the probationary period, which lasted nine months. The provost could, upon the advice of his consultors and the prefect, shorten the probation to six months or extend it to one year. During the time of probation the candidate was to make every effort to advance towards perfection. He was to give evidence of obedience and humility and to occupy himself in pious exercises and meditations which fostered the spirit of Christian discipline. The probationer was also exhorted to devote himself to study, the better to fit himself for instructing the people whom he would later serve.

Every three months during the period of probation two of the priests of the community were selected to examine the spiritual progress of the probationer and to make a report to the provost. Throughout the time of probation the aspirant was to receive

[2] *Institutionum ad Oblatos S. Ambrosii Pertinentium Epitome* (Mediolani: apud Dominicum Bellagattam, 1716), pp. 30–33.

nothing from the common goods of the community except food and other necessities.

At the close of the probation the candidate was to make a general confession of his entire past life. He then made the vow of obedience to the Archbishop, and became enrolled as an Oblate of St. Ambrose.

3. *The Congregation of Jesus and Mary*

The Constitutions of the Congregation of Jesus and Mary, which were approved by the Sacred Congregation of Bishops and Regulars on August 13, 1874, were substantially the same as those written by Saint John Eudes in 1652. The provisions which regulated the admission of candidates were set down in Part VI, Chapters I to XIV.[3]

The superior and those in charge in the Congregation were warned never to fall into the temptation to increase the number of members by relaxing the strict regulations set forth in the Constitutions. It was better, said the Holy Founder, to have a small community of pious and virtuous clerics than to have a large congregation of lax and worldly priests. Therefore great care and diligence had to be exercised in the admission of members.

The aspirant was to present himself at one of the houses of the Congregation where he was to be interviewed by the superior of the community and his assistants. The superior was to determine whether or not the applicant possessed the qualities required of those seeking admission: piety, sufficient learning and education, good health, unblemished reputation, a pleasant and sociable disposition, a spirit of humility and obedience, and a firm desire to consecrate his life to God.

Admission was to be denied to those who had ever been members or novices in any religious Order or congregation, to those who lacked respect for ecclesiastical authority, to persons of advanced age or to youths who were not yet sixteen years old, to those who had committed some great crime, to those who were burdened with debts, and to those who possessed a residential benefice.

---

[3] *Constitutions de la Congrégation de Jésus et Marie* (Amiens: Pitieux Frères, 1899), pp. 190–247.

Having carefully examined the postulant on all these points, the superior was then to instruct him regarding the nature, the purpose and the work of the Congregation. If he was satisfied that the applicant possessed all the required qualities, he was to write to the superior general, without whose permission no one could be received into the institute. When the superior general had approved the application, the postulant was to be sent without delay to the institute's house of probation.

Upon the arrival of the candidate at the house of probation (*maison des jeunes*), the director was to make a record of all that the postulant had brought with him, so that these might be returned to him in the event of his departure or dismissal. The aspirant was to enter immediately upon a ten-day spiritual retreat, during which he was to make a general confession of his past life. At the conclusion of the retreat he was invested with the habit of the probationers and received into their number. Notice of his reception was entered in a book kept for this purpose.

During the first year the probationer was not permitted to engage in any studies, but was to devote himself entirely to the development of his spiritual life. He was to assist at Mass every day (probationers who were priests were to offer the Holy Sacrifice daily); receive Holy Communion twice weekly; choose the director as his confessor; learn the ceremonies of the liturgy; wait at table and perform manual labor; assist at the community exercises; and attend the private and public conferences given by the director.

The director of the probationers was to be a priest renowned for his humility, charity and spirit of discipline. He was to give good example to the probationers. He was to foster in them a great esteem and reverence for their vocation, obedience to the Constitutions, and a respect for the spirit of the Congregation. He was to hold private conferences with them and give them his advice and counsel. Every three months he was to send a written report to the superior general and in it set forth his opinions on the qualifications and dispositions of each probationer.

At the conclusion of the first year of probation the director examined the probationer for the sake of ascertaining whether or not the latter was determined to persevere. He then made a report to the superior general.

With the consent of the superior general and his assistants, the probationer, at the end of the first year of probation, made the "*protestation*" of stability in the institute. Leaving the house of probation, he was sent to one of the colleges or seminaries of the Congregation, there to continue his studies. Probationers who were priests were assigned to a seminary or some other house. A director was assigned to the probationer to foster in him the spirit of piety and the practice of solid virtue. At the conclusion of the second year another examination was made with a view to ascertaining whether the probationer was still determined to persevere as a member of the Congregation.

The entire period of probation lasted three years and three months; it could be prolonged by the superior general if he judged that this was necessary. At the conclusion of this period the probationer could be admitted definitively as a member of the Congregation. It was necessary that the Fathers of the house first give their approval, and that this be communicated to the superior general. The consent of the latter having been given, the probationer entered upon a ten-day retreat, at the conclusion of which he made the final "*protestation*" or "*engagement*" of perseverance and stability in the institute, and thus became incorporated as a member of the Congregation of Jesus and Mary.

PART 2—CANONICAL COMMENTARY

CHAPTER VIII

THE CONCEPT OF A CANONICAL NOVITIATE

1. *The Purpose and Nature of the Novitiate*

The word *novitiate* is frequently used in designation of a religious house legitimately destined to receive those who must undergo probation before profession.[1] Juridically, it is a moral collegiate person, legitimately erected by competent ecclesiastical authority and specially designated for the training of novices.[2]

Formally considered, however, it is a state in which aspirants prepare themselves to embrace the religious life; they learn the rule and discipline of the community and try to discover whether they are capable of bearing the burdens of the religious life; the community, on the other hand, examines and tests their character, dispositions and abilities before admitting them to profession.[3]

The novitiate, therefore, comprises both a negative and a positive element. The negative element is found in the fact that the candidate has not made his profession. He is seeking admission into a community, and admission is brought about only by profession. Until the candidate has been actually professed, he has not achieved the end towards which he is striving. The mere fact that profession has not yet taken place is not, however, sufficient. A positive element is also required, and this consists in the candidate's offering himself to the community and the community's acceptance of the offering, both of which must be manifested by some external sign. This brings about a closer union with the community, a union which did not exist when the aspirant was not yet a novice. It gives the community the right to impose burdens and duties upon the novice; in the novice it begets an obligation to accept whatever is imposed upon him.

[1] Wernz-Vidal, *Ius Canonicum ad Codicis Normam Exactum* (7 toms. in 8 vols., Romae: apud Aedes Universitatis Gregorianae, Tom. III, *De Religiosis,* 1933), III, n. 274 (hereafter cited *Ius Canonicum*).

[2] Bakalarczyk, *De Novitiatu,* p. 4.

[3] C. 16, X, *de regularibus et transeuntibus in religionem,* III, 31.

It should be noted that the various exercises of the novitiate, the tests, trials and other probationary elements, are not the substance of the novitiate. They are the end and purpose of the period of probation. The substance is present when both the community and the novice are in such a state that satisfactory knowledge of each other can be obtained. It is conceivable that all the novitiate exercises might be omitted, that the community would make no effort to examine the character of the aspirant, and that the novice might deliberately neglect to study the rule and discipline of the community. Such a procedure would, indeed, be harmful to both parties, and the purpose of the novitiate would not have been attained. Nevertheless, it could not be argued that the subsequent profession would be invalid, for the substance of the novitiate is not found in positive acts of probation, but in the fact that the novice voluntarily remains in a state in which probation *can* be made.[4]

No definite period of probation is required by divine law for entrance into religion. All that is required is an examination of the candidate's vocation, his character and other circumstances which call for exploration. Once the examination has been made, the candidate may be admitted to the religious life without delay, and this was the usual procedure with the ancient hermits, solitaries and virgins.[5]

The introduction of the cenobitic type of monasticism, however, seemed to make some form of probation necessary, and the Rules of the early communities almost always provided for a trial period of some sort.[6] Even in the Rules there was no uniform time period for probation, and later general legislation did not prescribe the same length of probation for everyone.[7]

The Council of Trent prescribed a uniform one-year novitiate for all religious Orders under pain of invalidity for the subsequent

[4] Suarez, *Opera Omnia* (28 vols., ed. L. Vivès, Parisiis, 1856–1861), *De statu perfectionis et religionis,* Tract. VII, lib. V, c. 14, nn. 4, 7, 8—XV, 361–363.

[5] Suarez, *De statu perfectionis et religionis,* Tract. VII, lib. V, c. 12, n. 2 —*Opera Omnia,* XV, 356.

[6] *Regula Pachomii,* c. 49—*MPL,* XXIII, 70; *Regulae Fusius Tractatae, Interrogatio X,* XXXI, 943.

[7] *Glossa Ordinaria,* ad c. 1, c. XVII, q. 2, s. v. *unius anni.*

profession.[8] Later legislation made suitable dispositions regarding the time, place and discipline of the novitiate and the rights and privileges of novices.[9]

The purpose of the novitiate is the formation of the novices' character through the study of the rule and the constitutions, through pious meditations and assiduous prayer, through instruction in all matters pertaining to the vows and the cultivation of virtue, and through pious exercises conducive to the complete eradication of faulty habits, the control of the passions and the acquisition of virtues. Candidates for the lay brotherhood must, moreover, be diligently instructed in Christian doctrine.[10]

In order to assure proper dispositions for the exercises of the novitiate, novices are not permitted to indulge in any extensive studies of literature, of the sciences or of the arts. Novices who are priests are not allowed to preach, to hear confessions, or to attend to outside offices or functions of the religious community. Lay brother novices may, within the house of novitiate, attend to the duties and work done by lay brothers, but not as principal brothers in charge of offices, shops, etc., and only in so far as such work does not interfere with the exercises prescribed for them in the novitiate.[11]

The novitiate may be called *canonical* when it is prescribed by the general law of the Church; it is *constitutional* when prescribed by the constitutions of individual communities. For example, in communities which have two years of novitiate, the first is generally the canonical year, since it is mandatory upon all *religious* communities; the second year is constitutional, since provisions for the additional year are found in the constitutions of the community, but not in the general law.[12] The constitutional no-

---

[8] Sess. XXV, *de regularibus*, c. 15.

[9] Sixtus V, const. *Ad Romanum* 21 nov. 1588—*Fontes*, n. 164; Clemens VIII, const. *Regularis disciplinae*, 12 mart. 1596—*Fontes*, n. 183; Clemens VIII, const. *Cum ad regularem*, 19 mart. 1603—*Fontes*, n. 189; cans. 542–571.

[10] Can. 565, § 1, 2.

[11] Can. 565, § 3.

[12] Schaefer, *De Religiosis ad Normam Codicis Iuris Canonici* (3. ed., Romae: Typis Polyglottis Vaticanis, S. A. L. E. R., 1940), p. 465 (hereafter cited *De Religiosis*).

vitiate may be required either for the validity of the profession or simply for its lawfulness.[13]

2. *Age Requirements*

The Council of Trent, in setting a minimum age for valid profession, did not thereby set up any provisions for a minimum age for entrance into the novitiate.[14] It could seem from the wording of the legislation that profession was to follow immediately upon the conclusion of the novitiate, and that fifteen years completed was therefore the minimum age for entrance into the novitiate. Schmalzgrueber, however, disagreed with this inference and was of the opinion that the previous law regulating reception into the novitiate had been left unchanged, and that the novitiate could be entered at an age, even earlier than at the age of fifteen years.[15] Fagnanus reported that the Sacred Congregation of the Council inclined to the opinion that the Council of Trent did not intend to set any definite age for the valid reception of the religious habit.[16] It should be noted that Pope Clement VIII ordered that the constitutions of each community were to be observed in this matter.[17]

In 1632, however, the Sacred Congregation of Bishops and Regulars forbade the superior general of the Theatines to admit novices to the religious habit until they had completed their fifteenth year of age.[18] Although this letter was regarded as the norm regarding the proper age for beginning the clerical novitiate in the mind of the Holy See, the letter was clearly addressed to a particular community with a view to remedying a particular abuse, and therefore cannot be regarded as a general law.[19] Later, in 1675, the same Sacred Congregation issued a general decree in

---

[13] Can. 555, § 2.

[14] Sess. XXV, *de regularibus*, cc. 15, 16.

[15] *Ius Ecclesiasticum*, Lib. IV, tit. XXXI, n. 44.

[16] *Commentarium*, Lib. III, c. XVI, n. 14.

[17] Const. *Cum ad Regularem*, 19 mart. 1603, § 4—*Fontes*, n. 189.

[18] S. C. Ep. et Reg., decr. *Clericorum Regularium*, 16 iul. 1632—*Fontes*, n. 1742.

[19] Balzer, *The Computation of Time in a Canonical Novitiate*, The Catholic University of America Canon Law Studies, n. 212 (Washington, D. C.: The Catholic University of America Press, 1945), p. 107.

which it commanded that no one was to be invested in the religious habit until he had completed the fifteenth year of age. Lay brother candidates were not to be invested until they were at least twenty-one years of age.[20]

The Sacred Congregation of Religious abolished the difference in the required ages for clerical and lay candidates in the Decree *Sacrosancta* of January 1, 1911.[21] The general law of the Church now requires fifteen years completed as the minimum age for entrance into the novitiate, and makes no distinction between clerical and lay candidates.[22] An aspirant who has not yet completed fifteen years is invalidly admitted to the novitiate.[23]

The constitutions of religious communities or of societies of quasi-religious can require a higher minimum age for admission than that prescribed by the Code, for the Code legislates only concerning the minimum age. Many communities also set a maximum age for admission, and this too is permissible.[24]

3. *Continuity of the Novitiate Year*

The present legislation on the length and continuity of the probationary period is the natural outgrowth and development of many preceding papal enactments and laws. In the early centuries there was a variety of provisions regarding the length of the novitiate, and this matter was largely regulated by the particular law of the monastery or the institute. The Rule of St. Benedict had, of course, a wide influence, and in the West candidates for profession were generally given a year's training. But it was not until the thirteenth century that Alexander IV (1254–1261) issued the first piece of ecclesiastical legislation that brought the obli-

---

[20] Bizzarri, *Collectanea in Usum Secretariae Sacrae Congregationis Episcoporum et Regularium* (2. ed., Romae: ex Typographia Polyglotta S. C. de Propaganda Fide, 1885), pp. 274–275 (hereafter cited Bizzarri).

[21] *Acta Apostolicae Sedis, Commentarium Officiale* (Romae, 1909 ——), III (1911), 30 (hereafter cited *AAS*).

[22] Can. 555, § 1, 1°.

[23] Can. 542, 1°.

[24] Larraona, "Consultationes," *Commentarium pro Religiosis* (Romae, 1920–1934: ab anno 1935, *Commentarium pro Religiosis et Missionariis*), XVII (1936), 9, nota 154 (hereafter cited *CpR* and *CpRM* respectively).

gation as to the length of the novitiate within the scope of the common law.[25]

He commanded the Order of Friars Minor and the Order of Friars Preachers to observe a full year of probation under penalty of invalidity for the subsequent profession. Forty years later Boniface VIII (1294–1303) extended this legislation to all Mendicant Orders, and the Council of Trent with a general law finally extended it to all religious Orders. The Tridentine law gave definite emphasis to the necessity of at least one year of probation, adding once again the sanction of invalidity relative to the subsequent profession. This tradition continued until the promulgation of the Code, which has now canonized it. For the common law today echoes the law of the Council of Trent in prescribing an integrally complete and continuous year of probation under pain of nullity of both the novitiate and the subsequent profession.[26]

The Tridentine legislation was addressed directly to members of religious Orders with solemn vows. Congregations with simple vows were a later evolution of the religious state. Nevertheless, it has been the constant practice of the Sacred Congregations to apply the law of the Council of Trent to all religious institutes.[27] The *Normae* of 1901, which were directive norms to be followed in the founding of new religious institutes, very clearly prescribed that one year, continuous and integral, was absolutely prerequired in every religious institute for the validity of the subsequent religious profession.[28] The Code of Canon Law has, of course, definitely removed any doubts by making the one-year novitiate mandatory upon all *religious* institutes.

By making a full year of probation to be of the very form and substance of a valid profession, the Tridentine law implicitly sanctioned a careful computing of the year of novitiate. All the commentators agreed that the Conciliar Fathers demanded a year that was mathematically integral and complete, and also continuous, that is, exclusive of interruptions. The time involved,

[25] C. 2, *de regularibus et transeuntibus ad religionem,* III, 14, in VI°.

[26] Can. 555, § 1, 2°; can. 572, § 1, 3°.

[27] Wernz, *Ius Decretalium,* III, n. 633.

[28] *Normae secundum quas Sacra Congregatio Episcoporum et Regularium procedere solet in Approbandis Novis Institutis votorum simplicium* (Romae: Typis S. C. de Propaganda Fide, 1901), n. 72.

they contended, had to be computed from the moment the novitiate had begun. Even a brief voluntary departure from the religious house was generally regarded as constituting an interruption that demanded a repetition of the novitiate.[29]

This very strict interpretation of the method of computing the time of probation lasted until the year 1914. So many cases involving the validity of profession had come before the Holy See that the Church decided to relax the rigor of the method of time-computation then in use. Instead of the "natural reckoning," i.e., the moment to moment or mathematical computation that prevailed after the Council of Trent, the use of a "civil reckoning" was allowed. This meant that the old "hour to hour" computation was replaced by a less rigid "day to day" reckoning, in which the absences of mere fractions of days never invalidated the subsequent profession.

In accord with the whole relaxed tenor of the Decree of 1914[30] there appeared for the first time in this same document certain regulations with regard to interruptions of the novitiate year, which were substantially taken over by the Code four years later.[31] For the first time, for instance, one finds in this Decree the determination that an absence from the novitiate covering a period of more than thirty days resulted absolutely in a substantial interruption of the novitiate. The Decree also contained the first mention of the permissible number of days of absence from the novitiate house still compatible with the validity of the novitiate or of the profession—a revolutionary innovation in the history of the novitiate time-computation.

In communities whose constitutions require a two-year period of probation, the first is generally considered the canonical year. In answer to a request for interpretation, the Pontifical Commission for the Interpretation of the Code stated that an Apostolic indult is required for a reversal of the order, so that the second year of novitiate would become the year of the canonical novitiate.[32] If, however, the constitutions which have received ap-

[29] Balzer, *The Computation of Time in a Canonical Novitiate,* p. 121.

[30] S. C. de Religiosis, decr., 3 maii 1914—*Fontes,* n. 4419.

[31] Can. 556, § 2.

[32] Pont. Comm. ad Cod. Interpr., resp., 12 febr. 1935—*AAS,* XXVII (1935), 92.

proval after the Code expressly state that the first year is the constitutional and the second the canonical year, then the novitiate may be entered at any age prescribed by the constitutions, even though the age count be less than fifteen years completed.[33]

4. *The Novitiate House*

The novitiate must be spent in the novitiate house.[34] Canon 554 gives the rules for the legitimate erection of the novitiate house. Communities of pontifical approval must obtain permission of the Holy See in order to erect a house of novitiate, or to designate an already existing house as the novitiate, or to transfer the novitiate from one location to another. In communities of diocesan approval no permission of the Apostolic See is required by the general law, but the individual constitutions are to be observed. If the constitutions are silent on this point, the permission of the local ordinary should be secured.[35]

Common law requires that the novitiate be made in a legitimately erected novitiate house; if it is made in any house other than those mentioned above, the novitiate is invalid, and the subsequent profession also becomes invalid.

Summary

From what has been stated in the preceding articles, it can be seen that three elements are required by the general law of the Church for the validity of the novitiate:

1) The aspirant must be at least fifteen years of age completed;
2) The novitiate year must be entire and continuous; and
3) The novitiate must be made in a legitimately erected house of novitiate.

These three elements, in addition to a fourth, viz., that the

[33] Vermeersch-Creusen, *Epitome Iuris Canonici cum Commentariis ad Scholas et ad Usum Privatum* (6. ed., 3 vols., Mechliniae-Romae: Dessain, 1937–1946), I, 483 (hereafter cited *Epitome*); Coronata, *Institutiones Iuris Canonici ad Usum Utriusque Cleri et Scholarum* (ed. altera, 5 vols., Taurini: Marietti, 1939–1945), I, 709 (hereafter cited *Institutiones*).

[34] Can. 555, § 1, 3°.

[35] Beste, *Introductio in Codicem* (ed. altera, Collegeville, Minn.: St. John's Abbey Press, 1944), p. 369 (hereafter cited *Introductio*).

aforementioned provisions are required by the general law for the validity of the subsequent profession,[36] make the novitiate *canonical;* if one of these elements is lacking, the novitiate is constitutional only, for it does not fulfill the requirements of the common law.

The question now arises: Do societies of quasi-religious (canons 673–681) have a canonical novitiate? The answer must be in the negative, for nowhere in the Code is the novitiate prescribed for such societies. The only canon which enacts any legislation regarding the admission of candidates to such organizations is canon 677, and this canon does not even indirectly prescribe a year's period of probation, but merely directs that the constitutions of each community be observed.

However, the constitutions of many such societies indicate that a so-called novitiate is prescribed, and that it is necessary for a valid entrance into those societies. The prescriptions of Book II, Title XI, of the Code are taken over almost in their entirety and embodied in the constitutions of these societies. Certainly the Sacred Congregation of Religious, whose duty it is to approve the constitutions of religious and quasi-religious, has at least tacitly sanctioned the use of the word *novitiate* for describing the period of probation in these societies.

It seems reasonable to conclude, therefore, that when this is the case, the period of probation in quasi-religious societies can be called an *analogously* canonical novitiate. Of course, strictly taken, the novitiate in such communities, regardless of how much it resembles a strictly canonical novitiate, is still constitutional only, since the binding force of this legislation comes not from the general but from a particular law. But it is precisely because of its resemblance to a strictly canonical novitiate that one may conclude that it is analogously canonical.

The probation period in societies without vows is therefore analogously canonical when the constitutions prescribe:

1) That candidates have completed fifteen years of age;
2) That the period of probation extend for at least one year, complete and uninterrupted;

---

[36] Can. 572, § 1, 3°.

3) That the period of probation be made in a house legitimately erected for this purpose; and
4) That the fulfillment of these conditions is necessary for the validity of the profession or of entrance into the society.

If any of these requirements be lacking, the probation is then constitutional only, and not even analogously canonical.

CHAPTER IX

APPLICATION OF THE CONCEPT OF A CANONICAL NOVITIATE TO QUASI-RELIGIOUS SOCIETIES

As was noted in the previous chapter, four conditions must be present in order to justify the affirmation that the probation in quasi-religious societies is analogously canonical. These conditions are not found in the constitutions of all such societies. The constitutions of some, usually those which are missionary in character, allow a certain elasticity in regulations which pertain to the probation. Others incorporate the provisions of the general law almost in their entirety. The purpose of this chapter is to indicate the constitutions which provide for an analogously canonical novitiate, and those which make provision for a probation that is constitutional only. It should be noted that the list here given is not intended to be exhaustive, but has been compiled from constitutions which were made available to the writer.

1. Constitutions with Provisions for an Analogously Canonical Novitiate

a. The Congregation of the Mission

The novitiate in the Congregation of the Mission is known as the "*Seminarium Internum.*" It consists of a two-year period which must be preceded, in the case of lay brother candidates, by a postulancy of six months. Candidates who have not completed the fifteenth year of age are impeded from entrance into the "*Seminarium Internum.*" The two-year period must be continuous and complete, and made in a house lawfully erected for this purpose by the superior general and his council. These conditions are required for the validity of the probation, and a valid probation is necessary for the valid profession of the four *private* vows which are made by members of the Congregation.[1]

[1] *Schema Constitutionum Congregationis a Missione approbationi Conventus Generalis XXXI subjiciendum* (Lutetiae Parisiorum, 1947), nn. 145, 148, 149, 159 (hereafter cited *Schema Constitutionum, C. M.*)

b. The Society of the Catholic Apostolate

The Constitutions of the Society of the Catholic Apostolate (Pallottini), which were approved by the Sacred Congregation of Religious in 1910, make provisions for a novitiate very much like that which is prescribed by the Code. Persons who have not completed their fifteenth year cannot be validly admitted to the novitiate, and it is required for validity that one complete and continuous year be spent in the house of novitiate. The seat of the novitiate is fixed, or if necessary transferred, by the provincial or regional council, with the consent of the general council and the approval of the Holy See. First profession must be preceded by a valid novitiate.[2]

c. Missionary Priests of St. Paul the Apostle

The Constitutions of the Society of Missionary Priests of St. Paul the Apostle (Paulists) also show a marked similarity to the law of the Code. Fifteen years completed is the required age for admission to the novitiate. Noviceship must last for an entire and uninterrupted year in the novitiate house, which must be canonically established with the permission of the Holy See, and which can be transferred elsewhere only with its permission. A valid noviceship must precede the taking of the temporary promise by which admission is made into the society.[3]

d. Congregation of the Most Precious Blood

The Constitutions of the Congregation of the Most Precious Blood make similar regulations. Aspirants must be at least fifteen years of age, the probation must be made in a house of probation, and the period must last for a year, continuous and integral.

---

[2] *Constitutions of the Pious Society of Missions* (1935), nn. 31, 33. 68 (hereafter cited *Constitutions, P.S.M.*). The original title of the community founded by the Blessed Vincent Pallotti was "The Society of the Catholic Apostolate." However, it was considered too general and was later changed to "The Pious Society of Missions." In 1947, the Society petitioned the Holy See for a restoration of the original title and the request was granted. The Constitutions remain unchanged. In order to avoid confusion, the writer has retained, throughout this work, the title of the 1935 edition of the Constitutions of the Society.

[3] *Constitutions of the Society of Missionary Priests of Saint Paul the Apostle* (New York: The Paulist Press, 1942), nn. 13, 19, 20, 36 (hereafter cited *Constitutions, C. S. P.*).

Aggregation to the Congregation cannot be made until a valid probation has been completed.[4]

e. The Society of St. Joseph

The Constitutions of the Society of St. Joseph (Josephites), approved *experimenti gratia* in 1932, also conform to the Code provisions and refer to the period of probation as the novitiate. Candidates must be at least fifteen years of age, the novitiate must extend to an entire and continuous year, and must be spent in a canonically erected novitiate house. The house of novitiate cannot be erected or transferred without the deliberative vote of the general council and an indult of the Holy See. The novitiate must precede the temporary promise by which admission into the society is granted.[5]

f. Society of the Missionaries of Africa

The Constitutions of the Society of the Missionaries of Africa (White Fathers) were approved by the Sacred Congregation of the Propagation of the Faith in 1908. The novitiate in this society is of two years' duration. The first year is required for the validity of the oath by which admission is made to the society. Aspirants must be at least sixteen years of age, and the first year of novitiate must be spent in the novitiate house.[6]

g. The Congregation of Jesus and Mary

The probation in the Congregation of Jesus and Mary (Eudists) lasts for four years. It cannot be entered until the aspirant has completed the fifteenth year of age. The first year of probation must be made in a house of probation which has been authorized by the Holy See. Incorporation into the Congregation cannot be made until the probation has been completed.[7]

---

[4] *Regula et Constitutiones Congregationis Missionis a Pretioso Sanguine D. N. J. C.* (Carthagena, Ohio, 1946), nn. 128, 130, 133 (hereafter cited *Constitutions, C. PP. S.*).

[5] *Constitutions of the Society of St. Joseph of the Sacred Heart* (Rome: Vatican Polyglot Press, 1932), nn. 19, 56, 57, 79 (hereafter cited *Constitutions, S. S. J.*).

[6] *Constitutions de la Société des Missionaires d'Afrique* (Algiers: à la Maison Mère, 1938), nn. 139, 154, 158 (hereafter cited *Constitutions, W. F.*).

[7] *Constitutions de la Congrégation de Jésus et Marie* (Paris: Maison Généralice, 1928), nn. 13, 15, 18 (hereafter cited *Constitutions, C. J. M.*).

2. Constitutions with No Provisions for an Analogously Canonical Novitiate

a. The Society of St. Columban

The Constitutions of the Society of St. Columban, which were definitively approved by the Sacred Congregation of the Propagation of the Faith in 1932, provide for a probationary period of twelve months for priests and candidates destined for the priesthood, and twenty-four months for lay brother candidates. They demand that the prescriptions of canon 542 be observed, and hence aspirants must be at least fifteen years of age. It is not required, however, that the probation be made in a house set aside for this purpose, nor does it appear that a continuous period of probation is demanded. Hence the probation in this society is not an analogously canonical probation.[8]

b. The Catholic Foreign Missionary Society of America

The Constitutions of the Catholic Foreign Missionary Society of America (Maryknoll) likewise demand the observance of canon 542. All aspirants to membership in the society, whether as priests, students or lay brothers, must make a probation year before being allowed to take the oath which admits them to the society. The probation year is to be spent in a house or section of a house specially prepared for that purpose. The probation year is not, however, a *sine qua non* condition for admission into the society, since the Constitutions allow the superior general and his council to dispense from a part of the probation year when secular priests who belong to a mission of the society wish to become members.[9]

c. The Scarboro Foreign Mission Society

The Scarboro Foreign Mission Society has a period of probation which lasts for one year. It may be made at the Mother House

---

[8] *Constitutiones Societatis Sancti Columbani* (1932), nn. 8, 9, 11 (hereafter cited *Constitutions, S. S. C.*).

[9] *Constitutions of the Catholic Foreign Missionary Society of America* (2. ed., Maryknoll, N. Y., 1938), nn. 3, 147, 149, 151 (hereafter cited *Constitutions, M. M.*).

or at any other house of the society. Students may combine the year of probation with the scholastic year. The probation, therefore, does not resemble the canonical novitiate in any way.[10]

[10] *Constitutions of the Scarboro Foreign Mission Society* (Scarboro Bluffs, Ontario, 1941), nn. 12, 13, 14, 15, 22.

CHAPTER X

THE POSTULANCY IN QUASI-RELIGIOUS SOCIETIES

1. Nature of the Postulancy

The postulancy may be defined as a certain period of preparation and trial during which a candidate remains as a guest in some religious house before being admitted to the period of probation properly so called.[1] It therefore precedes the period of probation which must be made in the novitiate or house of probation, and was introduced in order that there might be furnished an ample opportunity for a preliminary acquaintance with the rule and customs of the institute. The present law of the novitiate concedes a certain incorporation into the community, as is evident from the fact that probationers enjoy all the spiritual favors which are accorded to the professed members, as well as certain other rights, but not all of these favors are granted to postulants, and hence the postulancy does not induce this incorporation.[2]

The general law of the Church does not require any period of postulancy for quasi-religious, male or female, clerical or lay. *De facto,* however, particular law, as found in the constitutions of the individual societies, in almost all cases makes some provision for a postulancy, at least with reference to candidates for the lay brotherhood.[3]

The postulancy is never demanded for the validity of the novitiate or of the subsequent profession, even in religious communities. It is not necessary for clerical candidates unless the constitutions so prescribe, for the entire period of their course of studies has the nature of a preparation for admission into the probation. Preparatory seminaries and Apostolic schools can, in a broad sense, be considered as postulancies.[4]

---

[1] Schaefer, *De Religiosis,* p. 451.

[2] Coronata, *Institutiones,* I, 705.

[3] Cf., e. g., *Constitutions, M. M.,* n. 179; *Constitutions, S. S. J.,* n. 113; *Constitutions, C. S. P.,* n. 9; *Schema Constitutionum, C. M.,* n. 144, § 2.

[4] Voltas, "Consultationes," *CpR,* II (1921), 221.

2. Duration of the Postulancy

In common law the postulancy, when prescribed, must last for at least six whole months,[5] and this is the usual period of the postulancy when it is demanded in quasi-religious societies. However, at least one such community, the Society of the Catholic Apostolate, demands only four months.[6] No special formality is required for admission into the postulancy, and hence the procedure in this matter will be determined by the constitutions or through the custom of the society. The constitutions or the approved usage will also determine the superior who is competent to receive the postulant, although this prerogative usually belongs to the major superior.

The period of time prescribed for the postulancy in religious communities must be complete, though not necessarily continuous, as is the case in the novitiate. The computation of time in a quasi-religious postulancy is not touched by the authors, but it appears reasonable to apply the same norms as those which are enforced in religious communities. Moral continuity is necessary, for the postulancy would defeat its purpose if it were broken up into several periods of time, each widely separated from the other. If a postulant had left the house with the intention of not returning, but upon a later decision has returned to the house, he could, in the opinion of Vermeersch-Creusen[7] and Fanfani,[8] conjoin the two periods of time as serving for the duration of his postulancy, provided that only a short time had intervened between his departure and return. As a practical norm, the period of absence should no longer be considered a brief interval if it has exceeded a duration of fifteen days.

Likewise, in the case of a postulant who has left the house for some just and grave cause, e.g., illness, and has persevered in his intention to continue his postulancy, the days need not be supplied, provided the time does not exceed fifteen days.[9] Several authors

---

[5] Can. 539, § 1.

[6] *Constitutions, P. S. M.*, n. 27.

[7] *Epitome*, I, 479.

[8] *De Iure Religiosorum ad Normam Codicis Iuris Canonici* (2. ed., Taurini-Romae: Marietti, 1925), p. 212 (hereafter cited *De Iure Religiosorum*).

[9] Schaefer, *De Religiosis*, p. 458.

also maintain that the superior can, for any just cause, shorten the time of the postulancy by fifteen days or less. A just cause would exist, for example, when it is desirable that all be received into the novitiate at the same time and this would not otherwise be possible unless the postulancy for one or the other were shortened. An absence for more than fifteen days, whether intermittent or continuous, should be regarded as implying a substantial interruption of the postulancy. Although the authors are speaking of the religious postulancy, it seems to the writer that analogically there is reason for the application of these norms to the quasi-religious postulancy as well.[10]

The major superior in a religious community is permitted to extend the time of the postulancy, but not beyond six months.[11] Some authors are of the opinion that through this prescription it is intended that the complete period must be limited in such a way that it never extends beyond one year.[12] Nevertheless, it seems more likely that if the constitutions prescribe a postulancy that is longer than six months, the major superior has the power to extend the duration of the postulancy for six more months, even though the total time would then exceed a one-year period.[13] The norm of canon 20 seems applicable here in such manner as to imply that the power to extend the time of the postulancy is enjoyed also by major superiors in quasi-religious societies.

3. Place of Postulancy

The postulancy may be made in the house of novitiate (or

---

[10] Schaefer, *De Religiosis, loc. cit.;* Bastien, *Directoire Canonique à l'usage des Congrégations à Voeux Simples* (3. ed., Bruges: Charles Beyaert, 1923), n. 79 (hereafter cited *Directoire Canonique*); Cappello, *Summa Iuris Canonici in Usum Scholarum Concinnata* (3 vols., Vol. II, 4 ed., 1945; Vol. III, 2. ed., 1940, Romae; apud Aedes Universitatis Gregorianae), II, 43 (hereafter cited *Summa*); Wernz-Vidal, *Ius Canonicum,* III, n. 242.

[11] Can. 539, § 2.

[12] Biederlack-Führich, *De Religiosis* (2. ed., Oeniponte: Rauch, 1919), n. 62; Augustine, *A Commentary on the New Code of Canon Law* (8 vols., Vol. III, St. Louis: Herder & Co., 1919), III, 203 (hereafter cited *Commentary*).

[13] Chelodi, *Ius Canonicum de Personis* (3. ed., curavit Pius Ciprotti, Vicenza: Libreria Moderna Editrice, 1942), n. 264 (hereafter cited *Ius de Personis*); Wernz-Vidal, *Ius Canonicum,* III, n. 242, nota (8).

house of probation) or in some other house of the society in which the discipline according to the constitutions is carefully and exactly observed. The postulants are to be under the care of a suitable member of the community.[14] The Sacred Congregation of Bishops and Regulars several times condemned the practice of sending postulants to a house in which discipline was not perfectly carried out,[15] but even if these admonitions were not observed, that fact did not in any way affect the validity of the postulancy,[16] and this would also now hold true, in the writer's opinion, even in quasi-religious societies, unless the constitutions stated otherwise.

If the postulancy is made in the house of formal probation or in the novitiate house, it seems more suitable that the master of novices (or director of probationers) should have charge of the postulants. Schaefer is of the opinion that, if the constitutions prescribe a postulancy for clerical candidates, they must be under the care and guidance of a priest,[17] but it does not appear that this could be imposed upon quasi-religious societies as a matter of obligation, although it would surely be more prudent to have a priest in charge of clerical postulants. The portion of the house set aside for postulants should, if conveniently possible, be separated from the section reserved for the probationers or novices.

4. Discipline of the Postulancy

No definite age is required by the general law for the valid or licit admission into the postulancy. The candidate should, nevertheless, be old enough so that, when the postulancy has been completed, he can be validly admitted into the probation. It is not necessary that the postulant be free from impediments which would prevent his reception into the probation,[18] nor is it required that he have the testimonial letters which are needed for entrance into

---

[14] Can. 540, § 1.

[15] S. C. Ep. et Reg., 6 iun. 1860—Bizzarri, p. 781; 23 mart. 1860—Bizzarri, p. 778; 11 iun. 1860—Bizzarri, p. 785.

[16] Coronata, *Institutiones*, I, 707.

[17] *De Religiosis*, p. 459.

[18] Larraona, "Consultationes," *CpR*, I, (1920), 180–181; Vermeersch, "Quaestiones de Codice Canonico," *Periodica*, IX (1921), (5).

the probation.[19] Therefore, if testimonial letters have not yet arrived, or if a dispensation has not yet been granted from the impediments mentioned in canon 542, it is permissible to receive the candidate into the postulancy.

The discipline of the postulancy is left to the judgment and discretion of the superior, unless the constitutions make some specific provisions. Postulants should not be subject to the same rigorous restrictions as the probationers. It appears that there is no objection to the practice of having the postulants perform some external works of the society or of allowing them to engage in study.[20] It is not necessary that the postulants wear any special habit, although this is not forbidden. Their garb should be of a modest nature, and different of course from that which is worn by the probationers.[21]

It does not seem to be unlawful, in the opinion of the writer, to exact a fee for the time spent in the postulancy, unless this is forbidden by the constitutions of the society, for the law governing religious in this matter[22] is not applicable to quasi-religious societies.

Postulants do not enjoy the spiritual privileges which are accorded to professed members and probationers, nor are they entitled to the suffrages prescribed for deceased members and probationers, unless the contitutions state otherwise, nor do they enjoy the common privileges of clerics which are extended to novices and probationers, even in quasi-religious societies.[23]

Since no juridic bond exists between the society and the postulant, the latter is free to leave at any time, and the competent superior is free to dismiss him whenever a just cause for such dismissal exists.

General law requires that postulants make a spiritual retreat of eight whole days before their reception into the novitiate. During this retreat they should, according to the prudent judgment of

---

[19] S. C. Ep. et Reg., decr. *Romani Pontifices,* 25 ian. 1848—Bizzarri, pp. 831–832; Chelodi, *Ius de Personis,* n. 264 (b).

[20] Vermeersch-Creusen, *Epitome,* I, 480.

[21] Can. 540, § 2.

[22] Can. 570, § 1.

[23] Cans. 614, 680; Schaefer, *De Religiosis,* p. 455, 1036.

their confessor, make a general confession of their entire past life.[24] It does not appear that this regulation must be observed in communities in which a postulancy is not prescribed by the common law,[25] and it therefore does not bind quasi-religious societies, nor is it obligatory upon clerical candidates who are about to be received into the novitiate, even in religious communities. However, in both cases the constitutions almost always demand a spiritual retreat before reception into the novitiate or probation.

The probation should ordinarily follow the postulancy, so that there exist a moral continuity between the two.[26] If reception into the probation must be delayed by reason of some just cause, the provisions of canon 1001, § 2, relative to the repetition of the spiritual exercises of the retreat should be applied.[27] If the delay extends beyond six months, the retreat must be repeated; if the delay is of less than six months' duration, the Ordinary should be consulted and his decision observed.[28]

---

[24] Can. 541.

[25] Vermeersch-Creusen, *Epitome,* I, 481.

[26] Fanfani, *De Iure Religiosorum,* n. 189, dubium I.

[27] Beste, *Introductio,* p. 359.

[28] Schaefer, *op. cit.,* p. 461.

CHAPTER XI

ADMISSION TO THE PROBATION

It has been pointed out that most of the legislation pertaining to the probation in quasi-religious societies is of a particular nature and is to be found in the constitutions of each individual society. However, the matter is not left completely untouched by the general law. Canon 677 prescribes that, in addition to the constitutions, the provisions of canon 542, which establishes impediments to the valid and licit reception into the novitiate, must also be observed by quasi-religious societies in the admission of candidates.[1]

In order to be received into the probation, it is necessary that the candidate be a baptized Catholic who is motivated by a proper intention, is capable of bearing the burdens of the religious life, and is not laboring under any impediment.[2] These impediments are invalidating if they render the probation and profession invalid; they are impeding if they make the probation and profession illicit without impairing their validity. They may derive either from the divine or the ecclesiastical law.

Some persons are excluded by the natural law from a valid reception into the probation or the religious life. Infants and those who are perpetually insane cannot validly enter religion.[3] Moreover, it would be highly imprudent to grant admission to those insane persons who have lucid intervals. The *impuberes* (boys under 14, girls under 12) are forbidden, both by the natural law[4] and the traditional ecclesiastical legislation,[5] to enter the probation, for they are still under the care of their parents. Vermeersch-

[1] Can. 677.—In admittendis candidatis serventur constitutiones, salvo praescripto can. 542.

[2] Can. 538.

[3] Cappello, *Summa,* II, 47.

[4] Biederlack-Führich, n. 65.

[5] C. 2, X, *de regularibus et transeuntibus in religionem,* III, 31.

Creusen[6] and Wernz-Vidal[7] proposed the opinion that, even though this dependency endures until the child has reached its majority, nevertheless canon 555 carries with it a tacit emancipation for the purpose of entering the probation once the minor has completed his fifteenth year. Slaves, because of the acquired rights of their masters, cannot be validly received without their master's consent.[8] Naturally, those who do not enjoy a good reputation or whose character is questionable must be refused admittance to the religious life.

All the prohibitions of the natural law as stated above seem unquestionably to be applicable also to quasi-religious societies.

1. Invalid Admission to the Probation

In addition to any impediments which may be established by the constitutions of individual societies,[9] canon 542, 1°, lists eight classes of persons who are invalidly admitted to the probation.

a. Heretics and Schismatics

Those who have given external manifestation of heresy or schism and have adhered to a heretical or schismatic sect cannot be validly received into the probation. To be excluded from admission, it is not necessary that such persons be members of a non-Catholic sect at the time of their reception. If they have, at any time of their lives, given their names to or publicly defended the teachings of any society which publicly or privately professes a doctrine contrary to the Catholic faith, they must be denied entrance into the probation.[10]

Larraona is of the opinion that actual enrollment as a member in such an organization must have taken place before the impediment arises.[11] He bases his conclusion on canon 2314, § 1, 3°, and on a response of the Code Commission which uses the word

---

[6] *Epitome,* I, 482.
[7] *Ius Canonicum,* III, n. 238.
[8] Wernz-Vidal, *loc. cit.*
[9] Cf., e. g., *Schema Constitutionum, C. M.,* n. 145.
[10] Cappello, *Summa,* II, 45.
[11] *CpRM,* XVI (1935), 430.

"*adscriptio.*"[12] Simple defection from the Catholic faith or mere internal adherence to heretical or schismatic teaching is not sufficient to give rise to the impediment.[13]

Larraona likewise holds that the words "*sectae acatholicae*" as used in canon 542, 1°, refer to every non-Catholic religious organization, whether it admits or denies the existence of God, whether it professes apostasy, atheism, pantheism or polytheism.[14] Vermeersch-Creusen, however, exclude adherence to Judaism or paganism from the scope of the canon.[15] Persons who have belonged to Masonic orders, secret societies and other groups which are not directly religious in character are not subject to the impediment.[16]

The impediment is not applicable to persons who have been born in heresy or schism and later have become converted to the Catholic faith, but only to those who have fallen away from the faith and joined a non-Catholic sect.[17]

b. Persons Who Are under Age

The minimum age for admission into the probation is fifteen years completed.[18] The age of the person is to be computed according to the provision of canon 34, § 3, 3°, since the moment from which the computation begins (*terminus a quo*) does not coincide with the beginning of the day, the first day is not to be counted in the computing of the age. A person, therefore, who was born on January 1, 1935, could not be validly received into the probation until January 2, 1950.

As has already been noted,[19] the Code legislates only concerning

---

[12] Pont. Comm. ad Cod. Interpr., resp., 30 iul. 1934—*AAS,* XXVI (1934), 494.

[13] Coronata, *Institutiones,* I, 708.

[14] *Loc. cit.*

[15] *Epitome,* I, 483.

[16] Oesterle, *Praelectiones Iuris Canonici* (Romae: apud Collegium S. Anselmi, 1931), p. 304 (hereafter cited *Praelectiones*); Schaefer, *De Religiosis,* p. 464.

[17] Pont. Comm. ad Cod. Interpr., resp., 16 oct. 1919—*AAS,* XI (1919), 477.

[18] Can. 555, § 1, 1°.

[19] Cf. *supra,* p. 53.

the minimum age for valid entrance into the probation. The particular constitutions could prescribe a higher minimum age, and could even set a maximum age limit for a person's valid reception as a novice.[20] In both these cases dispensations would have to be sought from the appropriate ecclesiastical superior.

If, even through error, a person were admitted to the probation before he has completed the fifteenth year of age, the admission would be invalid. However, several authors hold that, if the intention of both the superior and the probationer has continued, then a virtual admission takes place on the day the required age is attained, and when all other provisions of the law have been fulfilled the probationer may be validly admitted to profession.[21]

c. *Persons under Constraint of Force and Fear*

Persons who are compelled to enter a society by reason of force, grave fear or deceit, or who are admitted by a superior thus constrained, are invalidly received into the probation.

Acts of any kind performed by physical or moral persons by reason of extrinsic force which they are unable to resist are invalid.[22] If, for example, a person were threatened with loss of life if he did not enter the probation, his reception would be invalid. The same is true if the superior's life were threatened if he were to refuse to accept a candidate.

But even a relatively grave fear, though it be a purely reverential fear, is sufficient under canon 542, 1°, to give rise to this impediment; the fear must come from outside the person intimidated (*ab extrinseco*).[23] Intrinsic fear, e.g., of the wrath of God, is not included under the factors causing this impediment.[24] Fear

---

[20] Prümmer, *Manuale Iuris Canonici in Usum Scholarum* (5. ed. Friburgi Brisgoviae: Herder & Co., 1927), p. 271 (hereafter cited *Manuale*).

[21] Schaefer, *De Religiosis;* Wernz-Vidal, *Ius Canonicum,* III, n. 247; Regatillo, *Institutiones Iuris Canonici* (2 vols., Vol. I, 2. ed., 1946; Vol. II, 1942, Santander: Aldus), I, 365 (hereafter cited *Institutiones*); "*utile per inutile non vitiatur.*"—Reg. 37, R. J., in VI°.

[22] Can. 103, § 1.

[23] Cappello, *Summa,* II, 45.

[24] Oesterle, *Praelectiones,* p. 289; Wernz-Vidal, *Ius Canonicum,* III, n. 248.

which arises from threats of death, exile, disinheritance, beatings and paternal indignation, since these threats come from outside the person intimidated, is sufficient to render the reception into the probation invalid.[25]

Deceit or fraud exists when one is persuaded to perform an action by reason of deceitful tricks or other dishonest means. Fraud is practiced if the parents make their child believe that they had promised to God that he would enter religion when, in fact, they had made no such promise; so also, if someone falsely persuaded another that the latter had the evident signs of a divine vocation. If the candidate has concealed a disease or a family disgrace which he knew or suspected would certainly cause his exclusion from the society, then his reception is likewise invalid.[26] If in view of the anxious desire to obtain candidates the society made false promises, the candidates who entered the probation solely or principally in reliance on these false promises are invalidly received.[27]

The superiors mentioned in this provision of the canon are any physical, moral or collective persons who have competence over the admission of candidates to the probation. If a physical person has sole competence over the admission of aspirants and has suffered no force, grave fear or fraud, the impediment does not arise, even though the members of his council may have been influenced by these causes.[28]

Canon 2352 punishes with a non-reserved excommunication all persons who force another to embrace the religious life. In accord with the principle that penal laws must be interpreted strictly,[29] it may safely be stated that this canon is not applicable to quasi-religious societies.[30]

---

[25] Schaefer, *De Religiosis,* p. 469.

[26] Cappello, *Summa,* II, 46.

[27] Regatillo, *Institutiones,* I, 365; Berutti, *Institutiones Iuris Canonici* (6 vols., Vol. III, *De Religiosis,* Taurini-Romae: Marietti, 1936), III, 139 (hereafter cited *Institutiones*); Creusen, *Religious Men and Women in the Code* (4. Eng. ed., Milwaukee: Bruce, 1940), pp. 134–135 (hereafter cited *Religious in the Code*).

[28] Schaefer, *De Religiosis,* p. 469.

[29] Can. 19.

[30] Coronata, *Institutiones,* IV, 496; Cappello, *Summa,* III, 549; Ayrinhac,

d. Persons Barred in Consequence of Marriage

Married persons are invalidly received into the probation as long as they are subject to the bond of their marriage. It should be noted that the prescriptions of the law make no distinction between a consummated and an unconsummated marriage, nor do they make any reference to the consent or refusal of consent to the admission on the part of the other spouse. Its provisions are absolute: once the marriage has been contracted, the spouse cannot enter the probation without the permission of the Holy See. Of course, once the marriage bond is dissolved, through death or some other cause, the person does not need this permission.

Coronata,[31] Cappello [32] and Goyeneche [33] maintain that the impediment ceases when a decree of perpetual separation has been granted. They base their doctrine on the wording of canon 1130.[34] Other authors hold a contrary opinion.[35] These maintain that the impediment continues in effect as long as the marriage bond lasts. To the writer it appears that this latter doctrine presents a more probable claim to correctness. Cappello [36] and Mothon [37] admit that in practice recourse should be made to the Holy See.

e. Persons Barred in View of Religious Profession

All persons who are bound or have been bound by religious

Penal Legislation in the New Code of Canon Law (New York: Benziger Bros., 1936), p. 246.

[31] *Institutiones,* I, 710.

[32] *Summa,* II, 46.

[33] *Iuris Canonici Summa Principia de Religiosis* (Romae: Tip. Pol. "Cuore di Maria," 1938), p. 83 (hereafter cited *De Religiosis*).

[34] Can. 1130.—Coniux innocens, sive iudicis sententia sive propria auctoritate legitime discesserit, nulla unquam obligatione tenetur coniugem adulterum rursus admittendi ad vitae consortium; potest autem eundem admittere aut revocare, nisi ex ipsius consensu ille statum matrimonio contrarium susceperit.

[35] Schaefer, *De Religiosis,* p. 470; Prümmer, *Manuale,* p. 268; Wernz-Vidal, *Ius Canonicum,* III, n. 249; Fanfani, *De Iure Religiosorum,* p. 199; Pejška, *Ius Canonicum Religiosorum* (3. ed., Friburgi Brisgoviae: Herder & Co., 1927), p. 80.

[36] *Summa,* II, 46.

[37] *Traité sur l'État Réligieux* (Paris: Desclée, de Brouwer & Cie., 1922), p. 306 (hereafter cited *État Réligieux*).

profession are invalidly admitted to the probation. This impediment was first introduced through a Decree issued by the Sacred Congregation of Religious in 1909.[38] The prohibition originally applied only to institutes of men, but was later extended to religious institutes of women.[39]

The Decree also applied the impediment to persons who had been novices in a religious community, but this prescription was abrogated by the Code. The impediment arises for all who have, at any time, made a valid religious profession, whether this profession was temporary or perpetual, whether made in an institute of pontifical or diocesan approval, whether made in an Order or in a congregation.[40] It applies to religious who have been secularized or dispensed from their vows, as well as to those whose vows have expired through the lapse of the time for which they were binding.[41] All these persons need a dispensation from the Holy See in order to enter the probation in quasi-religious societies.

Since the law which is contained in the first section of canon 542 is of an invalidating character, it is to be interpreted strictly.[42] The words "*professionis religiosae*" must therefore be taken in a properly restricted sense. Since a promise or oath of perseverance or obedience, or also private vows such as those taken by members of the Congregation of the Mission, do not properly connote a religious profession, the impediment does not arise for those who have been members of quasi-religious societies, and they can be legitimately received into the probation of another quasi-religious society, or of a religious congregation or Order.[43] Likewise, they would not be impeded from readmission into the same society, unless the constitutions ruled otherwise.

---

38 S. C. de Religiosis, decr. 7 sept. 1909—*AAS,* I (1909), 700.

39 S. C. de Religiosis, declar. 4 ian. 1910—*AAS,* II (1910), 63.

40 Vermeersch-Creusen, *Epitome,* I, 485.

41 Schaefer, *De Religiosis,* p. 471.

42 Can. 19.—Leges quae poenam statuunt, aut liberum iurium exercitium coarctant, aut exceptionem a lege continent, strictae subsunt interpretationi.

43 Goyeneche, "Studia Canonica" ("De egressu e religione"), *CpR,* V (1924), 338; Beste, *Introductio,* p. 360; Cappello, *Summa,* II, 46; Wernz-Vidal, *Ius Canonicum,* III, n. 250; Coronata, *Institutiones,* I, 711; Berutti, *Institutiones,* III, 141.

The impediment is not applicable to those who have made religious profession in danger of death, for such a profession implies no other juridic effect than a participation in the spiritual favors and privileges of the community.[44]

It is appropriate at this point to advert to a recent Decree which refers to admission to the probation. On July 25, 1941, the Sacred Congregation of Religious and the Sacred Congregation of Seminaries and Universities issued a joint Decree which prescribed that before a person who has belonged by any title to a religious family may be admitted to a seminary, the ordinary must have recourse to the Sacred Congregation of Seminaries and Universities; likewise, before a person who has for any reason left a seminary may become affiliated with a religious family, the religious superior must have recourse to the Sacred Congregation of Religious. The appropriate Congregation will then communicate its decision to the religious superior or to the rector of the seminary, in accordance with the nature of the case.[45]

The proper interpretation of this Decree has created some problems. The obscurity has been partially alleviated through a private response given to the General of the Society of Jesus, in which it is stated that the Decree does not concern those who leave a seminary or college in order to embrace a life of perfection in some religious institute.[46]

Further clarification was given in a declaration of the late Cardinal La Puma (+ 1943), Prefect of the Sacred Congregation of Religious at the time when the Decree was issued. His declaration was printed in the *Commentarium pro Religiosis et Missionariis*,[47] and substantially republished in this country.[48] The

---

[44] S. C. de Religiosis, decr. 10 sept. 1912—*AAS*, IV (1912), 589; S. C. de Religiosis, decr. et resp. 30 dec. 1922—*AAS*, XV (1923), 156.

[45] S. C. de Religiosis et S. C. de Sem. et Univ. Studiorum, decr. 25 iul. 1941—*AAS*, XXXIII (1941), 371.

[46] S. C. de Religiosis, resp. 11 maii 1942—Bouscaren, *The Canon Law Digest* (2 vols., Milwaukee, Bruce, 1934–1943), II, 166 (hereafter cited *CLD*).

[47] XXIII (1942), 226–237.

[48] Frison, "Ex-seminarian and Novice: A Clarification," *The Jurist* (Washington, D. C.: The Catholic University of America, 1941–), VI (1946), 416–418.

declaration of Cardinal La Puma makes clear that the Decree does not strictly constitute a canonical impediment to admission into a religious institute. Furthermore, the terms " religion " and " religious family " apply to true religious communities in a canonical sense. Hence, societies whose members imitate the manner of life of religious by living in community under the government of superiors according to approved constitutions, but without public vows or with no vows at all, are not, according to the Cardinal,[49] included in the Decree.

However, Regatillo reports [50] that the Sacred Congregation of Seminaries and Universities informed the Archbishop of Toledo (Spain) on May 8, 1945, that the provisions of the Decree were applicable to a young man who had left the *Societas Operariorum Diocesanorum* (a quasi-religious society) and desired admission to the archdiocesan seminary. Regatillo draws the conclusion that the Decree is applicable to quasi-religious societies.[51]

However, it seems to the writer that Regatillo's conclusion is unwarranted. The response was private, and hence bound only those for whom it was given. In any event, it seems that at least a *dubium iuris* is created, and hence the Decree is not obligatory for quasi-religious societies.[52]

f. Persons Hindered because of Their Crime

Those who are menaced with punishment for the commission of a grave crime of which they have been or can be accused are also excluded from a valid admission into the probation, even in quasi-religious societies. This impediment was introduced by Sixtus V [53] in order to prevent criminals and delinquents from using the religious state as a shield with which they could ward off the just punishments of the law, for once they had entered the

---

[49] *CpRM,* XXIII (1942), 232-233.

[50] *Institutiones,* I, 369.

[51] *Loc. cit.*

[52] Canon 15.—Leges, etiam irritantes et inhabilitantes, in dubio iuris non urgent. . . .

[53] Const. *Cum de omnibus,* 26 nov. 1587—*Fontes,* n. 162; Const. *Ad Romanum,* 21 oct. 1588—*Fontes,* n. 164.

novitiate they could invoke the privilege of the clergy (*privilegium fori*) in order to escape trial before a civil court.

The delict from which the impending punishment arises may be a crime that implied a violation of either the civil or the ecclesiastical law. The mere possibility that one will be brought to judgment is not enough to constitute a "menace" as contemplated in canon 542, 1°, for a menace supposes the probability of the denunciation or of an unfavorable judgment. Canon 542, 1°, speaks of a grave crime as the kind of offense it contemplates. Hence, the danger of having to submit to a penalty for the violation of some police regulation would not render invalid the admission into the probation.[54]

Moreover, when punishment impends for a crime committed in violation of a civil law or decree whose enactment lacks justice in its support, the impediment does not arise.[55] Such would be the case of a priest threatened with punishment for having rightfully exercised his ministry in opposition to a prohibition of the secular law, or for having defended the rights of the Church against an unjust violation.

A person who has been tried and acquitted, or one who has already undergone the punishment, may be validly admitted to the probation.[56] A person is likewise free from this impediment if he has been accused or condemned for a crime which he did not actually commit.[57]

g. Persons Impeded through Their Promotion to the Episcopate

Bishops, whether residential or titular, even though they have only been preconized by the Roman Pontiff, cannot be validly received into the probation of religious institutes or quasi-religious societies. Vermeersch-Creusen remark that the impediment is based, for residential bishops, upon the bond of spiritual union which unites an ordinary with his diocese; for titular bishops, upon the reverence owed to the Roman Pontiff, who has selected them

---

[54] Creusen, *Religious in the Code,* p. 135.

[55] Schaefer, *De Religiosis,* p. 473.

[56] Goyeneche, *De Religiosis,* p. 83.

[57] Coronata, *Institutiones,* I, 711; Cappello, *Summa,* II, 46; Fanfani, *De Iure Religiosorum,* p. 199.

for such a dignity.[58] The preconizing of a bishop is an act of major importance (*causa major*), which is reserved to the Roman Pontiff. It is only logical that once the Roman Pontiff has acted, his selection should not be subject to possible nullification through any act of his subordinates.[59] A person is preconized as a bishop when the Holy See, by an authentic act, even though not yet made public, has appointed a man to the episcopate. The preliminary election made by a cathedral chapter, or the presentation made by the civil government, does not give rise to the impediment.[60] Bishops who have resigned in such a way that they no longer have title to any diocese are free to embrace the religious or quasi-religious state.[61]

h. Persons Impeded through the Bond of Service to the Holy See

Clerics who by a disposition of the Holy See are bound by oath to consecrate themselves to the service of their diocese or of the missions are, during the period for which the oath binds them, invalidly received into the religious novitiate or quasi-religious probation. The Code makes no distinction between clerics in major Orders and clerics in minor Orders; hence those who have received at least tonsure are included among the persons here in question.[62]

The common opinion holds that the oath here mentioned is not to be confused with the oath that is mentioned in canon 981, § 1, for the latter is required by the general law, and not from any special disposition of the Holy See.[63] It is generally held that this section refers principally to the oath taken by clerical students of the Pontifical mission colleges in Rome. The oath taken by them is usually of a temporary nature,[64] whereas the oath to serve in a diocese or mission, as regulated in canon 981, § 1, is made per-

[58] *Epitome,* I, 485–486.

[59] Can. 220.

[60] Goyeneche, *De Religiosis,* p. 84.

[61] Berutti, *Institutiones,* III, 142; Vermeersch-Creusen, *Epitome,* I, 486; Schaefer, *De Religiosis,* p. 474.

[62] Cf. Can. 950.

[63] Coronata, *Institutiones,* I, 712; Berutti, *Institutiones,* III, 142; Cappello, *Summa,* II, 47.

[64] Fanfani, *De Iure Religiosorum,* p. 200; Berutti, *Institutiones,* III, 143.

petually and is intimately connected with the canonical title of ordination. The impediment therefore does not bind clerics who have taken the oath prescribed by canon 981, § 1,[65] but only those who by a disposition of the Holy See have sworn to devote themselves to a diocese or mission. When the time for which the oath was taken has elapsed, the impediment ceases.

* * * * *

The impediments mentioned in this article are the only impediments which by the general law render admission into the probation invalid. But they are equally applicable to religious institutes and to quasi-religious societies. All pre-Code impediments have been abolished, although all earlier enacted impediments retain their force if they be still incorporated in approved constitutions. Invalid entrance into the probation renders the entire probation invalid, and hence the subsequent profession has no juridic effect. Ignorance of the existence of the impediments does not validate the admission into the probation, for invalidating and disqualifying laws operate independently of good or bad faith in the parties concerned.[66]

2. Illicit Admission to the Probation

In addition to any impediments established by approved constitutions, the general law determines other impediments to the licit admission into the novitiate [67] which, by reason of canon 677, are also applicable to the reception into the probation of quasi-religious societies.

a. *Clerics in Major Orders*

Clerics in major Orders are impeded from a licit admission into the probation without the knowledge of the local ordinary, or against his will if his objection is based on the serious loss to souls that their withdrawal would occasion, when that loss cannot by any means be otherwise counteracted.

The Church has always recognized the right of clerics freely to

---

[65] Oesterle, *Praelectiones,* p. 291.

[66] Can. 16, § 1.

[67] Can. 542, 2°.

embrace the religious state, but in the course of time it became apparent that provisions had to be made regarding the entrance of secular clerics into a religious institute. The norms which governed such cases were originally established by Benedict XIV (1740–1758).[68]

The prohibition enacted in canon 542, 2°, does not apply to clerics who are in minor Orders.[69] The ordinary spoken of is evidently the ordinary of the diocese in which the cleric has been incardinated. Most of the authors hold that the permission of the ordinary is not necessary, but that the cleric need only take counsel with him.[70] Augustine (1872–1943) however maintained that the positive consent of the ordinary is required.[71]

It appears to the writer that, in the case of admission into a quasi-religious society, this opinion can claim the greater probability in its favor. The reason is based on a Decree of the Sacred Congregation of the Propagation of the Faith, which stated that a cleric or secular priest could not aggregate himself to any community of secular priests without the permission of his bishop.[72] The term "community of secular priests" seems to have been used in contradistinction to communities whose members made profession of the three public vows of religion, and accordingly appears to have applied to societies of quasi-religious. The Decree further noted that the bishop must not deny permission without solid reasons, but that, if the greater good of the Church demanded that the cleric or priest serve in his diocese, the bishop could compel him to leave the community and to return to the service of the diocese, provided that he was still subject to the bishop.

This earlier disposition does not seem to be opposed to the provisions of canon 542, 2°. Authors hold that the need of the diocese is the only cause which would allow a bishop to deny

---

[68] Ep. *Ex quo*, 14 ian. 1747—*Fontes*, n. 374.

[69] Prümmer, *Manuale*, p. 272.

[70] Coronata, *Institutiones*, I, 713; Vermeersch-Creusen, *Epitome*, I, 487; Schaefer, *De Religiosis*, p. 477; Wernz-Vidal, *Ius Canonicum*, III, n. 254; Regatillo, *Institutiones*, I, 367; Cappello, *Summa*, II, 47.

[71] *Commentary*, III, 212.

[72] Decr., 17 apr. 1820—*Fontes*, n. 4715.

permission to a cleric or a priest to enter a religious institute,[73] and it seems justifiable to apply their conclusions to entrance into a quasi-religious society. In case of a dispute regarding the ordinary's judgment in the matter, the case would have to be referred to either the Sacred Congregation of the Council or the Sacred Congregation of Religious, both of which are equally competent to render a decision.[74]

b. Persons Burdened with Debts

Those who are burdened with debts which they are unable to pay are illicitly admitted to the probation. The debts must be of such gravity and of such a nature that the creditor would have a right to institute court action in order to collect them.[75] If the debts have been settled by some friendly agreement, or if the creditor has legally renounced his right to sue, the impediment ceases.[76]

If the society has agreed to assume the obligation of paying the debts, the aspirant may be admitted to the probation, but Prümmer (1866–1931) advised great caution in these cases.[77] Augustine argued that the society would not be allowed to pursue such a course of action, except in the case of minor debts, for an offer to discharge the heavy debts of the aspirant would imply alienation.[78] Moreover, if court action has already been taken and the debtor has been freed from all legal obligation of making payment, or if the debts have become uncollectible by reason of prescription, the impediment ceases to exist.[79]

If there is no hope that the debtor will ever be able to discharge his obligations, or if he can pay only part of his debts, or if his failure to join a society will expose him to probable danger of eternal damnation, the impediment still exists,[80] but there is a very

---

[73] Fanfani, *De Iure Religiosorum,* p. 200; Pejška, *Ius Canonicum Religiosorum,* p. 81.

[74] Vermeersch-Creusen, *Epitome,* I, 488.

[75] Wernz-Vidal, *Ius Canonicum,* III, n. 255.

[76] Berutti, *Institutiones,* III, 145; Regatillo, *Institutiones,* I, 367.

[77] *Manuale,* p. 272.

[78] *Commentary,* III, 213.

[79] Vermeersch-Creusen, *Epitome,* I, 488.

[80] Cappello, *Summa,* II, 48.

strong basis for seeking a dispensation.[81] The mere fact, however, that admission to the probation would be advantageous to the spiritual good of the aspirant would not be a sufficient reason for seeking a dispensation, for the good of the society would have to be preferred to the private good of the one seeking admission.[82]

c. Persons Charged with Administration

Persons who are under the obligation of giving an account or who are implicated in other secular affairs which may involve the society in lawsuits or other annoyances are illicitly admitted to the probation. This impediment was first introduced by Sixtus V in the Constitution *Cum de omnibus.*[83]

The nature of the affairs is of little importance with reference to this prohibition: they may be private or public. The president of a corporation, the executor of a will, or a public official would all be equally excluded from a licit admission. Once the person has withdrawn from a responsible position in the management of secular affairs or has resigned from public office, he may be received into the probation, provided there is no danger that the society will be subject to lawsuits or other inconveniences of a similar nature.[84]

d. Persons with Family Obligations

Children who are needed for the support of their parents or grandparents who are in grave need, and parents whose help is needed for the support and education of their children may not be licitly received into the novitiate of religious institutes or the probation of quasi-religious societies.

The Code here confirms the natural obligation which children have with regard to supporting their parents when they are in need.[85] This natural duty always takes precedence over any act which is not of obligation but of counsel only. If the impediment

---

[81] Oesterle, *Praelectiones,* p. 293.

[82] Schaefer, *De Religiosis,* p. 479.

[83] 26 nov. 1587—*Fontes,* n. 162.

[84] Wernz-Vidal, *Ius Canonicum,* III, n. 256; Coronata, *Institutiones,* I, 714.

[85] Pejška, *Ius Canonicum Religiosorum,* p. 82.

is to arise, the parents or grandparents must be in grave necessity. It is not possible to indicate a strict rule which will determine the existence of such a necessity; the judgment must be based on the circumstances of each case.[86]

If in consequence of a child's entrance into a quasi-religious society a parent would be forced to undergo inconveniences which do not befit his state in life, a grave necessity would certainly exist in such a case.[87] The same would hold true if the parent were forced to seek refuge in a hospice for the indigent, and this would result in shame and loss of respect. All aspects of the case would have to be prudently judged before the existence of the impediment could be ascertained. Vermeersch-Creusen remarked that, when the necessity is not grave, but the entrance of the child would give rise to many inconveniences on the part of the parents, delay in entrance should be counselled.[88]

A candidate who is bound to help his parents or grandparents may freely enter the religious or quasi-religious life if he would be unable to help them even if he remained in the world, or if the other children are able and willing to help them, or if his remaining in the world would place him in grave and probable danger in the matter of gaining salvation.[89]

Although it is not specifically mentioned by the Code, authors generally hold that the impediment also exists when brothers and sisters are in *extreme* necessity.[90]

e. Clerical Candidates Canonically Impeded

Candidates for the priesthood who suffer an irregularity or some canonical impediment[91] cannot be licitly received into the probation of a clerical quasi-religious society. This section of canon 542, 2°, seems to imply that the impediment must be

[86] Fanfani, *De Iure Religiosorum,* p. 201.

[87] Berutti, *Institutiones,* III, 145.

[88] *Epitome,* I, 489.

[89] Regatillo, *Institutiones,* I, 368; Cance, *Le Code de Droit Canonique, Commentaire succinct et pratique* (7. ed., 3 vols., Paris: Gabalda et Cie., 1946), II, 62.

[90] Biederlack-Führich, *De Religiosis,* n. 74; Cappello, *Summa,* II, 48; Raus, *Institutiones Canonicae* (2. ed., Parisiis: Vitte, 1931), p. 296.

[91] Cans. 984; 985; 987.

removed or a dispensation obtained before the aspirant may be admitted into the probation. Failure to do so might offer prejudice to the judgment of the Holy See by presuming that a dispensation will be given when the time for the conferral of Orders arrives.

Fanfani [92] and Goyeneche [93] are of the opinion that an aspirant may be licitly admitted if the irregularity or the impediment is of such a nature that a dispensation is readily given. Authors generally agree that if there is certainty that the impediment or the irregularity will no longer exist at the time of the conferral of Orders, the candidate may be received into the probation apart from the obtaining of a dispensation.[94] It should be noted that a dispensation given for entrance into the probation is not simultaneously valid as a dispensation for the reception of Orders. A new dispensation should be sought at that time.[95]

f. Members of the Oriental Rite

Members of the Oriental rite are illicitly received into the probation of a quasi-religious society of the Latin rite without the written permission of the Sacred Congregation of the Oriental Church. This impediment does not affect those Orientals who have legitimately transferred to the Latin rite, nor those who seek admission into a society of the Oriental rite, nor those who, without changing their rite, are to be prepared to establish houses and provinces of their own rite.[96] If an Oriental wishes to enter a Latin rite probation, the Sacred Congregation of the Oriental Church has jurisdiction over such matters, but the candidate must observe the directions of the Sacred Congregation of the Propagation of the Faith [97] in petitioning the necessary permission.[98]

* * * * *

[92] *De Iure Religiosorum*, p. 203.

[93] *De Religiosis*, p. 86.

[94] Voltas, "Consultationes," *CpR*, II (1921), 368–370; Vermeersch-Creusen, *Epitome*, I, 490; Cappello, *Summa*, II, 49; Pejška, *Ius Canonicum Religiosorum*, p. 82.

[95] Vermeersch-Creusen, *Epitome*, I, 491.

[96] Pont. Comm. ad Cod. Interpr., resp. 10 nov. 1925—*AAS*, XVII (1925), 583.

[97] Ep. circ., 15 iun. 1912—*AAS*, IV (1912), 534.

[98] Berutti, *Institutiones*, III, 148.

Those who have been invalidly received into the probation need not necessarily be expelled. A dispensation should be sought and the time of probation should then be computed from the moment at which the dispensation was granted. A sanation might also be obtained and in this case the entire probation would be both valid and licit.[99] In no case, however, does an illicit admission render the novitiate or probation invalid, unless the candidate has fraudulently concealed the existence of some impediment.[100]

Canon 2411 directs that superiors who receive candidates into the probation in violation of canon 542 are to be punished according to the gravity of their guilt, even with deprivation of office. It has been authentically declared that this prescription of canon 2411 is also applicable to quasi-religious societies.[101] Punishment may be administered by the competent religious superior, by the ordinary of the place, or by the Holy See.

3. The Competent Superior

Canon 543 prescribes that the right of admitting candidates to the religious novitiate belongs to the major superiors with the vote of their council or chapter. This vote may be deliberative or advisory, according as the constitutions provide.

This canon is not inherently (*per se*) applicable to quasi-religious societies. The determination of the competent superior, as well as the nature of the vote of the council or chapter, should be resolved by the constitutions. However, if the constitutions fail to make provisions on this important point, it is necessary to rely on the prescriptions of canon 20 in order to supply for the lacuna in the law.

Wernz-Vidal stated[102] that the very nature of entrance into a society demands the consent of those who preside over that society. It is only reasonable to presume that some superior must have competence over the admission of candidates, and therefore by analogy with canon 543 this competence belongs to major superiors, unless the constitutions make other provisions. The supreme

[99] Vermeersch-Creusen, *Epitome,* I, 491; Coronata, *Institutiones,* I, 716.

[100] Schaefer, *De Religiosis,* p. 485; Beste, *Introductio,* p. 363.

[101] Pont. Comm. ad Cod. Interpr., resp. 3 iun. 1918—*AAS,* X (1918), 347.

[102] *Ius Canonicum,* III, n. 261.

moderator exercises this faculty for the entire society; provincial or regional superiors, for their province or region.[103] This is in accord not only with the general law, but also with the constitutions of many quasi-religious societies,[104] and *a pari* should be observed by societies whose constitutions are silent on this point.

In religious institutes the power of the superior is not absolute, but the vote of his council, either deliberative or advisory, is necessary. Coronata [105] and Larraona [106] maintain that pre-Code constitutions which gave this faculty to the superior alone are abrogated on this point and must be brought into agreement with canon 543; if this is not done, they say, all admissions which the superior grants on his own initiative are invalid. Prümmer also maintained that pre-Code constitutions are abrogated on this point, unless the right of admitting candidates is conceded to the superior alone by reason of a non-revoked privilege.[107] In the opinion of the writer, application of the authors' conclusions to quasi-religious societies is not warranted, and hence pre-Code constitutions of such societies which concede to the superior alone the right of admitting candidates remain in force.

The vote of the council when prescribed by the constitutions is, if it be characterized as deliberative, necessary for validity; [108] if it be termed simply advisory, it is probably not necessary for validity. The vote must be given by the members acting as a collegiate body, and hence the superior would not be permitted to ask the opinion of each individual councillor separately, but must consult the body as a whole.[109]

The nature of the vote of the council members must be determined by the constitutions. In some societies it is deliberative; [110] in others it is only advisory.[111] If the constitutions,

---

[103] Wernz-Vidal, *loc. cit.*

[104] Cf., e. g., *Constitutions, C. S. P.*, n. 12; *Schema Constitutionum, C. M.*, n. 143; *Constitutions*, P. S. M., nn. 29, 348, 11°.

[105] *Institutiones*, I, 716.

[106] "Consultationes," *CpR*, I (1920), 368.

[107] *Manuale*, p. 274.

[108] Can. 105, 1°.

[109] Coronata, *Institutiones*, I, 717.

[110] Cf., e. g., *Constitutions, C. S. P.*, n. 12; *Constitutions, S. S. J.*, n. 205, (g); *Constitutions, S. S. C.*, n. 6.

[111] Cf., e. g., *Constitutions, C. PP. S.*, n. 132; *Constitutions, S. M. A.*, n. 10.

while prescribing the vote of the council, do not determine the nature of the vote, it must be presumed to be consultative only.[112]

The right of admitting candidates to the probation does not belong to the Ordinary, even in societies that are of diocesan approval, unless this faculty is granted to him by the constitutions or by way of special privilege.[113] Some authors are of the opinion that the constitutions cannot give this power to the Ordinary because of the fact that, since he is not a religious superior, it would be contrary to the common law.[114] However, a reply of the Code Commission stated that the bishop or his delegate may be regarded as the legitimate superior for the receiving of the profession whenever the constitutions concede this power to him,[115] and hence it seems that the conclusions of the authors cannot be sustained in the present consideration which is of like import.

4. Testimonial Letters

Testimonial letters are documents which when given by the competent ecclesiastical authority help to inform major superiors of the qualities of a candidate and of his juridic capacity for admission into religion.[116] They are not demanded by the general law for societies whose members do not take public vows.[117] Particular law, as found in the constitutions, regulates this matter for quasi-religious. If the constitutions are silent on this matter, certain provisions of the general law should be observed, since the purpose of the testimonial letters is to insure that only those of good character will be received into the religious life. Certainly

---

112 Vermeersch-Creusen, *Epitome*, I, 200; Coronata, *Institutiones*, I, 188; Beste, *Introductio*, p. 162.

113 Goyeneche, *De Religiosis*, p. 80; Oesterle, *Praelectiones*, p. 297; Regatillo, *Institutiones*, I, 370; Berutti, *Institutiones*, III, 150.

114 Creusen, *Religious in the Code*, p. 139; Larraona, "Commentarium Codicis," *CpRM*, XVIII (1937), 321.

115 Pont. Comm. ad Cod. Interpr., resp. 1 mart. 1921—*AAS*, XIII (1921), 177.

116 Schaefer, *De Religiosis*, p. 487.

117 Cappello, *Summa*, II, 99; Cocchi, *Commentarium in Codicem Iuris Canonici ad Usum Scholarum* (8 vols., in 5, Liber II, Pars II, *De Religiosis* [Vol. IV], 3. ed., Taurinorum Augustae: Marietti, 1932), IV, 294 (hereafter cited *Commentarium*).

the Church is equally solicitous for the welfare of quasi-religious societies, and is therefore desirous that unworthy candidates should not be admitted into such organizations. Recourse must therefore be had to the general law as governing religious, in order to remedy the lack of a specific provision which could lead to disastrous results.

Hence, all those who seek admission into a quasi-religious society should present documents which prove that they have received the sacraments of baptism and confirmation. This is in harmony with canon 538, which is, in the opinion of the writer, analogously applicable to quasi-religious.[118] To argue that proof of the reception of baptism and confirmation is not necessary for aspirants to membership in societies without public vows, solely because they are not required by general, or perhaps particular, law, seems juridically unwarranted.

If the candidate has not yet been confirmed and will not be able to receive the sacrament except upon a lengthy and burdensome delay, it is permissible to receive the candidate, provided that every care is taken to see that the sacrament is administered to him as soon as possible.[119] This conclusion, made in regard to admission to religious institutes, is entirely justified in relation to admission to quasi-religious societies.

If the constitutions make some provision for the presentation of testimonial letters, even though they do not require all the letters mentioned in the general law governing religious,[120] no additional letters need be presented. If the constitutions are completely silent on this point, it appears that, for the sake of prudence and caution, all the letters demanded by canon 544 should be obtained, though this cannot be urged as a matter of obligation. In the first case the legislator has evidently felt that his provisions suffice to prevent the entrance of unworthy candidates; in the second case the provisions of the ecclesiastical law should be observed in order to prevent any violation of the natural law which denies admission to those whose character is questionable.

---

[118] Can. 538.—In religionem admitti potest quilibet catholicus qui nullo legitimo detineatur impedimento rectaque intentione moveatur, et ad religionis onera ferenda sit idoneus.

[119] Vermeersch-Creusen, *Epitome,* I, 494; Beste, *Introductio,* p. 364.

[120] Can. 544.

In addition to what is required by the general law or the constitutions, superiors are free to demand any other documents which may seem necessary or useful in attaining this end.[121]

* * * * *

It should be noted that the provisions of the articles in this Chapter are equally applicable in the admission of candidates to societies which have no formal period of probation.

[121] Can. 544, § 6.

CHAPTER XII

THE INTERNAL GOVERNMENT OF THE PROBATION

1. The Beginning of the Probation

The determination of the exact time at which the probation begins is of practical importance, for in individual cases it must be certainly and publicly evident when the probation commences, lest any doubts arise regarding the completeness and continuity of the probation period. The matter is usually settled by the constitutions. In some societies the probation begins when a declaration to this effect is made by the director or master of probationers;[1] in others, when the candidate is enrolled by the director of probationers in the official register of the probation;[2] in others, by the reception of the habit.[3]

If the probationers wear a habit different from that of the professed members, the probation usually begins with the reception of the probationers' habit. Berutti is of the opinion that this is the norm to be followed whenever the constitutions make no other provisions,[4] although the constitutions could make provisions for reception into the probation in some manner other than by investiture in the habit. Suppose, however, that the members and probationers of a quasi-religious society wear no distinctive habit but follow the mode of dress of the secular clergy, and the constitutions do not establish any definite time for the commencement of the probation. The matter is not touched by the authors, but it seems that then the custom of the society must operate in establishing the time when the probation begins.

Canon 557 prescribes that during the entire period of the religious novitiate there must be worn the habit which the constitutions prescribe for the novices. This provision is not

---

[1] Cf., e. g., *Schema Constitutionum, C. M.*, n. 149.

[2] Cf., e. g., *Constitutions, C. S. P.*, n. 21.

[3] Cf., e. g., *Constitutions, P. S. M.*, n. 33; *Constitutions, W. F.*, n. 153.

[4] *Institutiones*, III, 167.

applicable to probationers in quasi-religious societies, unless the constitutions so state, for the general law does not apply the above-mentioned canon to such societies. If no special habit is prescribed for the probationers, any manner of vesture will suffice.

2. The Place of Probation

The probation is ordinarily spent in the house of probation or in a part of some house of the society which has been specially set aside for the training of the probationers.

Societies of quasi-religious are bound to follow the law of religious regarding the erection and suppression of houses and provinces.[5] The permission of the Holy See and of the Ordinary, given in writing, is required for the erection

1) of an exempt religious house, whether fully organized or juridically inchoate;
2) in places subject to the Sacred Congregation for the Propagation of the Faith, of any religious house, even of an institute which has received but diocesan approval.[6]

In all other cases the permission of the Ordinary is sufficient for the erection of a religious house, whether the institute is of diocesan or pontifical approval. Therefore, the Ordinary's permission suffices for the opening of houses of quasi-religious societies.

Canon 554, § 1, demands the permission of the Holy See for the erection of the novitiate houses of religious institutes of pontifical approval. This canon is not applicable to quasi-religious societies for two reasons: 1) Quasi-religious societies are not true religious institutes, since their members do not take the three public vows of religion; 2) The probation in such societies is not a novitiate strictly so-called, and the house where the probation is made is not, juridically considered, a novitiate house, but a house of probation.

Therefore, for the erection of the house of probation no permission is required except that which is necessary for the erection of any other house of the society, and the consent of the Ordinary

[5] Can. 674.

[6] Can. 497, § 1.

suffices for the establishment or the transfer of the house of probation. Although true religious communities of pontifical approval need a special Apostolic indult in order to have more than one novitiate house in each province,[7] it is the opinion of the writer that, for the same reasons as those mentioned in the paragraph above, and in the absence of any specific legislation on this point, such an indult is not necessary for quasi-religious societies, and recourse to the Holy See would not have to be made for the erection of additional houses of probation in the same province, even though the society is of pontifical approval. It should be emphasized, however, that the provisions of the constitutions in this regard must of course be followed.

Unless the constitutions provide otherwise, the probation can be made in any house of the society, even though not specially designated as a house of probation. The constitutions can provide under pain of invalidity that the probation be spent in a designated house of probation. This is always the case in societies which have an analogously canonical period of probation.[8]

The living accommodations of the probationers need not exist separate from that part of the house which is occupied by the professed, although this is required in the novitiates of religious institutes.[9] Nevertheless, inasmuch as a full and easy association with the other members of the community would generally bring about a somewhat relaxed discipline, it seems wise that the constitutions incorporate some legislation which assigns separate quarters to the probationers. The wisdom of such a procedure seems evident; indeed, it seems necessary if the achievement of the purpose of the probation is to be successfully attained.

For similar reasons the lay brother candidates need not be separated from the clerical probationers, unless the constitutions make other provisions. Still, because of the widely divergent nature of the states to which they aspire, it seems the part of prudence to have separate quarters for those who aspire to clerical and lay membership in the society.[10]

---

[7] Can. 554, § 2.

[8] Cf. p. 57, *supra.*

[9] Can. 564, § 1.

[10] Can. 564, § 2.

In societies in which the candidates may aspire either to clerical or to lay membership, the probation which is made for one class will be valid for the other, unless the constitutions determine otherwise. This is not true in the case of religious institutes, for the general law demands the repetition of the novitiate if a candidate passes from one class to the other.[11] In the absence of any statement by the commentators, it seems to the writer that a strict interpretation must be given to this canon, and that in consequence it is not applicable to societies in which the three public vows of religion are not taken.[12]

Lest the religious training of the lay brother candidates be neglected, it seems that there should be incorporated in the constitutions the provisions of the general law which demand that they be diligently instructed in Christian doctrine, and that a special conference be given to them once every week.[13] This could not, however, be urged as a matter of strict obligation unless the constitutions so determined.

3. Time Computation of the Probation

a. *Time Computation in Societies Having an Analogously Canonical Probation*

In considering the method of the time computation of the probation, one necessarily must make a very clear distinction between probations that are analogously canonical and those which are not.[14]

Societies whose constitutions demand a complete and continuous year of probation as a necessary requirement for the validity of the profession must follow the law which governs the religious on this point.[15] Sometimes the provisions of the Code regarding the length, continuity and permissible interruptions of the religious novitiate are incorporated *verbatim* in the constitutions of such

---

[11] Can. 558.

[12] "Odia restringi, et favores convenit ampliari."—Reg. 15, R. J., in VI°.

[13] Can. 565, § 2; Pius XI, ep. ap. *Unigenitus Dei Filius*, 19 mart. 1924 —*AAS*, XVI (1924), 147.

[14] Cf. pp. 56–57, *supra*.

[15] Can. 556.

quasi-religious societies,[16] and the interpretations to be given to these provisions must, in accordance with canon 18, follow the interpretations given to the law which governs the factor of time-computation in religious novitiates. Even if such a literal transfer of the Code prescriptions were not found in the constitutions, canon 20 would nevertheless demand the application of similar legal norms in order to prevent a *lacuna legis* and to ensure an accurate computation of the year of probation, whenever it is required for the validity of the profession.

b. Time Computation in Societies Not Having an Analogously Canonical Probation

If, however, a complete and continuous year of probation is not required by the constitutions for the validity of the profession, it appears to the writer that a less rigorous method of time-computation becomes available for interpreting the constitutional provisions. Although the question is not touched by the commentators, it seems properly warranted to invoke and apply the law of the Code as it regulates the consideration of the time element with reference to the postulancy in religious institutes. The similarity between the two is readily apparent: both are required only for the licitness of the profession; neither is required by the general law of the Church for clerical aspirants; the binding force of any legislation in these matters (for clerical aspirants) is drawn entirely from the particular law; the validity of the profession remains unimpaired if either the postulancy or the probation period is omitted, unless the constitutions state otherwise.

It must not be presumed, however, that the probation, when imposed by the constitutions, is not of grave obligation, even though it be not prescribed for the validity of the subsequent profession. The gravity of the fault of such an omission must be determined by the constitutions, and any superior who disregarded the constitutional norms regarding the fulfillment of the prescribed time could be guilty of grave fault.[17]

---

[16] Cf., e. g., *Constitutions, S. S. J.*, nn. 58–59; *Constitutions, C. S. P.*, n. 22.

[17] Balzer, *The Computation of Time in a Canonical Novitiate*, p. 97; Creusen, *Religious in the Code*, p. 132.

Authors generally hold that the period of postulancy must be computed according to the norm given in canon 34, § 3, 3°, which is also the norm used in the computation of the year of the *religious* novitiate.[18] In the absence of any other criterion, it appears best to use this method of time computation for the probation in quasi-religious societies.

By use of the civil reckoning, as outlined in the cited canon, the time of probation should be so computed that the first day of the period is not reckoned, and the required period terminates with the last day of the same date twelve or more months later, according as the constitutions demand. The first day is not counted, for whenever according to the civil reckoning, by some act or formality recognized by law, the starting point of the period of time in question does not coincide with the very beginning of the natural day, the remainder of the first day is disregarded. The legal computation of the time begins only after midnight of the first day which in part the probationer has spent within the house to which he was assigned for the probation. It is obvious that the candidate would not normally begin his probation in the middle of the night.

Likewise, according to the same method of computation, the period of the probation ends with the completion of the very last day of the same date, i.e., on the same date (twelve or more months later, according as the constitutions prescribe) of the month in which the period took its legal beginning. For example, if a candidate began his probation at nine o'clock in the morning on the 1st of March, the actual legal or civil computation of the time would begin only after midnight of the first day spent in the house of probation, i.e., it would begin on the 2nd of March. If the probation were of twelve months' duration, it would end on the 1st of March, but only at the very last moment of that day, i.e., at midnight.

It is the common opinion of the authors that the time spent in the postulancy need not be of continuous duration. They allow minor interruptions and require only a moral continuity.[19] It

---

[18] Pont. Comm. ad Cod. Interpr., resp. 12 nov. 1922—*AAS,* XIV (1922), 661.

[19] Vermeersch-Creusen, *Epitome,* I, 479; Schaefer, *De Religiosis,* p. 457;

appears to the writer that the same norm should be applied to the time computation in the probation of societies which do not demand a complete and continuous year of probation as a requirement for valid profession.

Since the common law does not make it obligatory to supply for an absence of no more than fifteen days from the religious novitiate, and since the commentators apply this concession also to the period of the postulancy, it appears that a like absence does not, in any case, substantially interrupt the probation, and that accordingly there is no obligation of supplying the days that were lost.[20] Berutti extends this concession to twenty days.[21] If the aspirant has left the house with the intention of not returning, but nevertheless has within a short time returned, the probation need not be recommenced. It will be permissible to conjoin the two periods of time for the purpose of one and the same probation.[22] Beste remarks that such procedure is not permissible if the absence has been protracted beyond fifteen days.[23]

If, however, the aspirant has been absent for a period of between fifteen (twenty days, according to Berutti) and thirty days, with the permission of his superior and along with the intention of returning to the probation, it seems necessary to have recourse to canon 556, § 2, which demands the repetition of all the days which were spent outside the novitiate house. An absence of more than 30 days continuous, or intermitted, breaks the moral unity and completeness of the year and necessitates a repetition of the probation.[24]

Most of the authors agree that the duration of the religious postulancy may be shortened by a few days, and it appears reasonable to apply the same generous provisions to the probation in societies whose constitutions do not demand a complete and continuous year of probation under pain of invalidity for the

---

Coronata, *Institutiones,* I, 706; Chelodi, *Ius de Personis,* n. 264, nota (5); Berutti, *Institutiones,* III, 133; Cocchi, *Commentarium,* IV, 132.

[20] Cappello, *Summa,* II, 43.

[21] *Institutiones,* III, 133.

[22] Vermeersch-Creusen, *Epitome,* I, 479; Schaefer, *De Religiosis,* p. 458; Fanfani, *De Iure Religiosorum,* p. 211.

[23] *Introductio,* p. 358.

[24] Berutti, *Institutiones,* III, 133.

ensuing profession.[25] A just and reasonable cause must, of course, exist. Such would be the case if the probationer's entrance into the major seminary would have to be long delayed if he were forced to complete the entire period of probation.

The commentators cited in this section make their statements in regard to the religious postulancy, but it seems entirely justifiable, for the reasons stated above,[26] to apply their conclusions to the probation in quasi-religious societies whose constitutions do not demand a complete and continuous year of probation for a valid profession. Although the period of probation is usually of greater duration than the religious postulancy, nevertheless Berutti remarks [27] that his conclusions are warranted even when the constitutions of religious institutes demand a longer postulancy than one of six months, and hence it seems equally warranted to apply the authors' conclusions to the quasi-religious probation.

4. The Director of Probationers

The requirements for the office of director of probationers must be determined by the constitutions. The provisions of the common law regarding the master of novices [28] are not applicable to quasi-religious societies.

In spite of this, it is evident that the director, because of the great responsibilities entrusted to him, should be a person of prudence, charity and piety, and conspicuous for his observance of the rule of the society. He should have a proper acquaintance with the needs and requirements of the society, and this seems to postulate his membership in the society for some extended period of time. Although he need not necessarily be a priest, it is proper that in clerical societies, as in religious institutes,[29] the office of director of probationers, for both the clerical and lay candidates,[30] should be entrusted only to one who has received the priesthood.

---

[25] Bastien, *Directoire Canonique*, n. 79; Coronata, *Institutiones*, I, 706; Schaefer, *De Religiosis*, p. 457.

[26] Cf. p. 96, *supra*.

[27] *Loc. cit.*

[28] Cans. 559; 560.

[29] Can. 559, § 1.

[30] Fanfani, *De Iure Religiosorum*, p. 232; Wernz-Vidal, *Ius Canonicum*, III, n. 283.

The constitutions may also make provision for the appointment of an associate director, who can assist the director in the training of the probationers, and replace him whenever he is absent from the house. Lesser requirements seem postulated with reference to him than with reference to the one who holds the office of director, and he need not be a priest.[31] Both should be free from any tasks which would impede them in the discharge of their proper duties. The length of their terms of office should be determined by the constitutions, and they should not be removed without a just and grave reason. Re-election may be permitted.

Coronata maintains [32] that the constitutions of religious institutes which forbid re-election of the master of novices are abrogated on this point, but it does not appear that his conclusion is applicable to quasi-religious societies. No one should be assigned to the house of probation who is not conspicuous for his observance of the discipline of the society.[33]

The director of probationers has the grave obligation to instruct the candidates in all that is required by the constitutions. This duty is to be properly that of the director alone, and no one else should interfere in any way except those persons to whom this privilege is conceded by the constitutions. The director as well as the probationers should be subject to the superior of the house in which the probation is made. This prescription of the common law,[34] although directed to the master of novices in religious institutes, appears to the writer to be applicable to the director of probationers in societies without vows, in view of the very nature of his office.

The probationers are subject to the director and are bound to obey him by reason of the dominative power which he exercises.[35] The constitutions should provide for a report to be made to the major superior regarding the character, habits and abilities of each probationer.[36] If the constitutions are silent on this point, such a manner of action cannot be demanded as a matter of obligation.

---

[31] Goyeneche, *De Religiosis,* p. 101.

[32] *Institutiones,* I, 739.

[33] Can. 554, § 3.

[34] Cans. 561, § 1; 562.

[35] Can. 501, § 1.

[36] Can. 563.

5. Rights and Duties of Probationers

The purpose of the period of probation should be stated in the constitutions. Generally regarded, its aim in quasi-religious societies is quite similar to the purpose of the religious novitiate, i.e., the spiritual development of the candidate. As in the novitiates of religious institutes, this is usually fostered by means of pious meditations and assiduous prayer, and through various other exercises which tend to root out vices and develop the practice of the virtues.[37]

Since the purpose of the probation is also to prepare the candidate for admission into the society, he should receive a copy of the rule and constitutions of the community, in order that he may gain a full acquaintance with the manner of life that he intends to embrace. Bastien (1866–1940) reported[38] that the Sacred Congregation of Religious frequently insisted that a complete copy of the rule and constitutions be given to novices in Orders and religious congregations, and that a digest or summary was insufficient. It appears to the writer that a similar course of action should also be followed in quasi-religious societies, although in the absence of any legislation specifically directed to such societies this could not be urged as a matter of obligation.

In the novitiates of religious the novices are forbidden by the general law to preach or to hear confessions (if they are priests), to engage in the external works of the institute, or to devote themselves to a serious study of the arts, the sciences or literature; lay brother candidates are permitted to perform the tasks usually assigned to the lay brothers, but not as officials in charge of others, and only in so far as such activities do not interfere with the novitiate exercises.[39]

This provision of the Code is not strictly applicable to probationers in societies without vows, and the writer has been able to discover no author who says that it is analogously applicable to them. However, it is evident that these activities could offer serious prejudice to the attainment of the purpose of the probation. It appears, therefore, that such activities should not be permitted

[37] Can. 565, § 1.

[38] *Directoire Canonique,* n. 129.

[39] Can. 565, § 3.

if they interfere in any way with the fulfillment of the constitutional provisions regarding the aim of the probation period. Indeed, the constitutions of many quasi-religious societies incorporate these provisions of the general law and apply them to their probationers.[40]

Several authors are of the opinion[41] that the current legislation in the Code for novices in religious institutes does not mean to prevent them from all exercise of the sacred ministry or from all study of science, arts or letters, but expresses the intention of the legislator that these activities be kept secondary and subordinate to the chief aim of the novitiate, which is the development of the spiritual character of the aspirant. Beste is of the opinion that one hour's daily study of Latin, Greek or one's native tongue, and instruction in sacred chant or in public speaking is desirable for clerical novices. He bases his view on a pre-Code Decree of the Sacred Congregation of Religious which, though it is no longer preceptive as law, can nevertheless serve as a directive norm.[42] It appears entirely justifiable to apply the same norm to probationers in quasi-religious societies.

A later Instruction of the same Sacred Congregation directed the supreme moderators of communities of lay religious to provide for the suitable instruction of the probationers in Christian doctrine during the probation period.[43] This Instruction employed the words *probandatus* and *tyrones* along with the more common *novitiatus* and *novitii,* and this may furnish reason for believing that the Instruction was also intended as applicable to quasi-religious societies. However, the Instruction is addressed "*ad supremos moderatores et moderatrices religiosarum laicarum familiarum,*" and hence it appears to the writer that its provisions cannot be imposed, except as a matter of counsel, upon societies whose members do not take public vows.

The provisions of canon 566, § 1, regarding the confessions of

---

[40] Cf., e. g., *Constitutions, S. S. J.*, n. 69; *Constitutions, C. S. P.*, n. 25; *Constitutions, P. S. M.*, n. 48.

[41] Vermeersch-Creusen, *Epitome,* I, 508; Fanfani, *De Iure Religiosorum,* p. 225; Wernz-Vidal, *Ius Canonicum,* n. 286; Beste, *Introductio,* p. 376.

[42] S. C. de Religiosis, decr. 27 aug. 1910—*Fontes,* n. 4405.

[43] S. C. de Religiosis, instr. 25 nov. 1929—*AAS,* XXII (1930), 28–29.

female novices are not directly applicable to female probationers in quasi-religious societies. However, since the legislation regarding the confessions of professed female members of religious institutes [44] is also applicable to the professed female members of quasi-religious societies,[45] and since the legislation is of a favorable nature, it is the opinion of the writer that the extension of canons 520–527 to include the female probationers of quasi-religious societies within their scope is not without warrant.[46] It should be noted also that the confessors of female professed members and female probationers of quasi-religious societies do not need the special jurisdiction which is demanded by canon 876, § 1, for the valid and licit reception of the confessions of the female professed members and female novices of religious institutes.[47]

For the same reasons as those mentioned in the preceding paragraph, it may be concluded that the special regulations of canon 566, § 2, regarding the confessions of male novices in religious institutes are not to be applied to male probationers of quasi-religious societies, but that their confessions are regulated by canons 518, 519 and 529.

The duties of the probationers should be determined by the constitutions. Although the professed members of quasi-religious societies are bound by the common obligations of clerics as enacted in canons 124–142,[48] it does not seem proper to extend these obligations to members who are not yet professed, since "*favores convenit ampliari, et odia restringi.*" [49]

Schaefer (+ 1948) stated explicitly that the probationers enjoy the common privileges of clerics as outlined in canons 119–123,[50] as well as other privileges directly granted to the society, but not the privileges of religious unless these have been granted to them by indult, for not even the professed members of the society

[44] Cans. 520–527.

[45] Can. 675.—". . . in omnibus serventur, congrua congruis referendo, can. 499–530."

[46] " Odia restringi, et favores convenit ampliari."—Reg. 15, R. J., in VI°.

[47] Berutti, *Institutiones*, III, 368.

[48] Can. 679, § 1.

[49] Reg. 15, R. J., in VI°.

[50] *De Religiosis*, p. 1036.

enjoy them.[51] They therefore enjoy the privileges of the canon, of the forum, of immunity and of competence.

Probationers may not be promoted to Orders during the period of probation. This prohibition arises not from canon 567, § 2, which is directed only to novices in religious communities, but from the Instruction *Quantum Religiones* of the Sacred Congregation of Religious.[52] Another prohibition, contained in canon 964, § 4, forbids the promotion to major Orders of subjects whose vows are only temporary. In the opinion of Coronata [53] this same prohibition is applicable to quasi-religious. The prohibition enacted in the Instruction *Quantum Religiones* has reference to both major and minor Orders, and also to the reception of the clerical tonsure. Professed members of quasi-religious societies may not be promoted to major Orders until three years after their first profession or aggregation to the society, and even then only when perpetual profession or aggregation to the society has been made.

The constitutions must determine the mode of procedure to be followed in regard to the disposition of the temporal goods of the probationers. In some societies the members make a promise of poverty, whose extent and binding force must be established by the constitutions. In others, the members retain both title to and use of their temporal goods. The probationers should be encouraged to make a last will and testament, although this is not obligatory as it is for novices in institutes whose members take the three public vows of religion.[54]

In the opinion of the writer it seems permissible, in the absence of constitutional restrictions, to exact a fee for the time spent in the probation, for the law governing religious in this matter [55] is not applicable to quasi-religious societies. If the probationer leaves the society, justice demands the restitution of all the tem-

---

[51] Can. 680.

[52] S. C. Religiosis, instr. 1 dec. 1931—*AAS,* XXIV (1932), 74–81.

[53] *Institutiones Iuris Canonici, De Sacramentis* (3 vols., Taurini-Romae: Marietti, 1943–1946), II, 56.

[54] Can. 569, § 3.

[55] Can. 570, § 1.

poral goods that he brought with him and has not consumed by use.

Regarding the dowry of female probationers, the provisions of the individual constitutions govern the matter completely.

The probationer is free to leave the society at any time, and he may be dismissed for a just cause by the superior or by the chapter, according to the constitutions, apart from any revelation of the causes of the dismissal.[56] Although this provision of the general law is not applicable to quasi-religious, and although the matter is not discussed by commentators, it seems that by analogy it should be observed. A contrary interpretation, so it appears to the writer, would be alien to the mind of the Church and opposed to the very purpose of the probation period. Berutti states [57] that a just cause for dismissal can be any defect of a physical, intellectual or moral nature affecting a quality which is required for the attainment of the general and special purpose of the community.

Upon the completion of the period of probation the aspirant is usually admitted to profession. If the candidate has been found unsuitable, he should be dismissed. If there is doubt regarding the fitness of the candidate, the general law allows major *religious* superiors to extend the time of the *novitiate,* but not beyond six months.[58] No such liberty is accorded by the general law to the superiors of quasi-religious societies, although such provisions are frequently found in individual constitutions. The point is not touched by authors, but it is the opinion of the writer that, by analogy, such permission can be extended to societies without vows in the absence of contrary restrictions in their constitutions. The society is entitled to have full knowledge of the character and abilities of the candidates it receives; if such knowledge has not been obtained within the prescribed period of probation, it seems that a prorogation may be permitted, unless the constitutions state otherwise.

Since a prorogation is also permitted by commentators in those religious institutes in which the regular noviceship is of more than

---

56 Can. 571, § 1.

57 *Institutiones,* III, 192.

58 Can. 571, § 2.

one year's duration,[59] it appears that their conclusions can also be applied to quasi-religious societies in which the regular period of probation extends beyond twelve months. Regatillo remarks that the religious novitiate may be extended even for some external cause, such as military service or sickness, and that the time of prorogation in this case is not limited to a six-month period,[60] but Jombart holds that in this case an Apostolic indult would be needed for a prorogation beyond six months.[61] Although both authors are speaking of religious institutes, their conclusions may be applied, by analogy, to quasi-religious societies.

Since, as Bakalarczyk (1885–1948) remarked, the nature of the religious novitiate is such that it is a preparation for profession,[62] and since the quasi-religious probation is also a preparation for incorporation into the society,[63] it seems reasonable to apply his conclusion to such societies by holding that profession or aggregation should follow without delay upon completion of the period of probation.

If, after having completed the full period of probation, the probationer has been unjustly dismissed, or has been forced to leave the house of probation (e.g., because of war, revolution or epidemic), but returns within a short time and seeks admission to profession, there is no need to repeat the probation.[64] Voltas[65] adds to this case a qualification, viz., that no great change shall have meanwhile occurred either in the candidate or in the society, and that the candidate shall not have been absent for an excessively long period of time. In these circumstances, he says, the probation must be repeated. It should be noted that Voltas gives no indication of what he considers to be an excessively long period of time.

---

[59] Coronata, *Institutiones*, I, 749; Bastien, *Directoire Canonique*, n. 116; Berutti, *Institutiones*, III, 192.

[60] *Institutiones*, I, 378.

[61] "Consultations" ("Profession Retardée par la Maladie"), *Revue des Communautés Réligieuses* (Louvain: Museum Lessianum, 1925–), V (1929), 76–77.

[62] *De Novitiatu*, p. 194.

[63] Cf. p. 101, *supra*.

[64] Beste, *Introductio*, p. 382.

[65] "Quaestio Canonica," *CpR*, II (1921), 81.

If the probationer has been justly dismissed or has left spontaneously upon the completion of the full period of probation, the question of his readmission is more difficult to solve. Beste [66] and also Voltas [67] discuss this hypothesis. Voltas points out that the older authors always demanded a repetition of the probation in the event that the character of the aspirant had undergone a great change, or if the nature of the institute had been radically altered. If, however, such is not the case, then according to Voltas a probation of six months would be allowable and sufficient for profession. There seem to be no compelling reasons for objecting to this manner of procedure, since, as has been noted above,[68] the superior enjoys the power to extend the probation for six months. It appears to the writer that an entire new probation could not be demanded, since the period of probation, once validly completed, can never be invalidated by any subsequent action of the will. It would perhaps be better to follow the suggestion of Beste who advises that, since the matter is doubtful, it should be submitted to the Holy See for a solution.

Although the authors who are cited in the two preceding paragraphs directed their remarks to religious institutes, it seems justifiable to apply their conclusions to quasi-religious societies, as the writer has done.

Novices in communities of religious are bound to make a spiritual retreat of eight whole days before profession.[69] This legislation does not apply to quasi-religious, unless the constitutions so state. If the constitutions are silent on this point, profession may validly and licitly be made without a retreat, though the performance of such spiritual exercises is certainly to be encouraged.

---

66 *Loc. cit.*

67 *Loc. cit.*

68 Cf. p. 105, *supra.*

69 Can. 571, § 3.

CONCLUSIONS

A brief recapitulation of the principal conclusions reached in the foregoing study may be stated as follows:

1. Since the early cenobites did not take the customary three public vows of religion, they may rightfully be considered as distantly foreshadowing the quasi-religious societies of modern times.

2. The legislation governing quasi-religious societies is drawn largely from particular, rather than general, law.

3. The general law of the Church does not prescribe a postulancy or novitiate on the part of those who aspire to membership in quasi-religious societies.

4. If the constitutions of a quasi-religious society require a period of probation, it may be considered as an analogously canonical novitiate if the constitutions prescribe:

   a) that candidates must have completed fifteen years of age;
   b) that the period of probation extend for at least one complete and uninterrupted year;
   c) that the period of probation be made in a house legitimately erected for this purpose; and
   d) that the fulfillment of these conditions is necessary for the validity of the profession or of entrance into the society.

5. All the impediments enacted in canon 542 are equally applicable to quasi-religious societies, even if they have no period of formal probation.

6. The prohibitions of the natural law against entrance into a religious institute are also applicable with reference to entrance into a quasi-religious society.

7. Canon 2352, which punishes with excommunication all persons who force others to enter a religious institute, does not refer to entrance into a quasi-religious society.

8. The impediment of religious profession, as stated in canon 542, 1°, does not refer to those who have made profession in a society whose members do not take the three public vows of

religion. Such persons can be legitimately received into the probation of another quasi-religious society, or readmitted into the same society; they can likewise be received into the novitiate of a religious congregation or Order.

9. The joint Decree of the Sacred Congregation of Religious and of the Sacred Congregation of Seminaries and Universities of July 25, 1941, does not bind quasi-religious societies.

10. A cleric in major Orders must obtain the permission of his Ordinary if he desires to leave his diocese and enter a quasi-religious society.

11. The section of canon 2411 which prescribes the punishment for superiors who violate the prescriptions of canon 542 in the reception of candidates is applicable to the superiors of societies without vows.

12. The designation of the superior who is competent to receive aspirants into the probation should be resolved by the constitutions; if the constitutions are silent on this point, this power belongs to the supreme moderator for the entire society, and to the provincial or regional superior in his province or region.

13. The right of admitting candidates into the probation of quasi-religious societies does not belong to the Ordinary, even in societies that are of diocesan approval, unless the faculty is granted to him by the constitutions or by way of special privilege.

14. Testimonial letters required by the constitutions must be presented by the aspirants; if the constitutions do not require any testimonial letters, prudence and caution direct that all the letters demanded by canon 544 should be obtained, though this cannot be urged as a matter of obligation.

15. The probation need not be spent in a special vesture or habit unless the constitutions so provide.

16. For the erection of the house of probation no permission is required by the general law other than that which is required for the erection of any other house of a quasi-religious society. An Apostolic indult is not necessary for the erection of additional houses of probation in the same province, unless such an indult is required by the constitutions.

17. In the absence of constitutional restrictions the probation may be made in any house of the society, and there is no need of

maintaining for the probationers quarters which are separate from those of the professed members, or quarters which for those who aspire to the clerical state are separate from the quarters of those who aspire to lay membership in the society. The probation made for the one class is valid for the other, unless the constitutions provide otherwise.

18. Unless the constitutions require a complete and continuous year of probation as a requirement for the validity of the profession, the probation of quasi-religious societies requires only a moral continuity.

19. The requirements for the office of master of novices in religious institutes are not applicable to the director of probationers in quasi-religious societies, unless the constitutions so state.

20. No special instruction in Christian doctrine need be given to the lay probationers during the period of probation, unless the constitutions so direct.

21. The confessions of female probationers in societies without vows are regulated by the provisions of canons 520–527; confessors of female quasi-religious, professed or probationers, do not need the special jurisdiction mentioned in canon 876, § 1. The confessions of male probationers in societies without vows are regulated by the provisions of canons 518, 519 and 529.

22. Probationers enjoy the common privileges of clerics; they are not bound by the common obligations of clerics.

23. Probationers in quasi-religious societies may not be promoted to Orders during the period of probation.

24. The major superiors in quasi-religious societies have the power to extend the period of probation, but not beyond six months, unless the constitutions make other provisions.

BIBLIOGAPHY

SOURCES

Acta Apostolicae Sedis, Commentarium Officiale, Romae, 1909- .

Bizzarri, A., *Collectanea in Usum Secretariae Sacrae Congregationis Episcoporum et Regularium,* 2. ed., Romae, 1885.

Bouscaren, T. L., *The Canon Law Digest,* 2 vols., Milwaukee: Bruce, 1934-1943.

Bullarum Diplomatum et Privilegiorum Sanctorum Romanorum Pontificum Taurinensis Editio, 25 vols., Augustae Taurinorum, 1857-1872.

Butler, Cuthbert, *Sancti Benedicti Regula Monasteriorum, Editio Critico-Practica,* 2. ed., Friburgi Brisgoviae: Herder & Co., 1927.

Codicis Iuris Canonici, Pii X Pontificis Maximi iussu digestus, Benedicti XV auctoritate promulgatus, Romae: Typis Polyglottis Vaticanis, 1917.

Codicis Iuris Canonici Fontes, cura Eñi Petri Card. Gasparri editi, 9 vols., Romae (postea Civitate Vaticana): Typis Polyglottis Vaticanis, 1923-1939 (Vols. VII-IX ed. cura et studio Eñi Iustiniani Card. Serédi).

Concilii Tridentini Diariorum, Actorum, Epistularum, Tractatuum, Nova Collectio, 13 vols., Friburgi Brisgoviae: Herder & Co., 1901-1938. Vol. IX, *Pars Sexta Actorum,* collegit, illustravit, edidit Stephanus Ehses, 1924.

Constitutiones Societatis Sancti Columbani, 1932.

Constitutions de la Congrégation de Jésus et Marie, Amiens: Pitieux Frères, 1899.

Constitutions de la Congrégation de Jésus et Marie, Paris: Maison Généralice, 1928.

Constitutions de la Société des Missionaires d'Afrique, Algiers: à la Maison Mère, 1938.

Constitutions of the Catholic Foreign Mission Society of America, 2. ed., Maryknoll, N. Y., 1938.

Constitutions of the Pious Society of Missions, 1935.

Constitutions of the Scarboro Foreign Mission Society, Scarboro Bluffs, Ontario, 1941.

Constitutions of the Society of Missionary Priests of Saint Paul the Apostle, New York: The Paulist Press, 1942.

Constitutions of the Society of St. Joseph of the Sacred Heart, Rome: Vatican Polyglot Press, 1932.

Corpus Iuris Canonici, Editio Lipsiensis 2a, 2 vols., Richter-Friedberg, Lipsiae, 1879-1881. Editio anastatice repetita, 1922.

Corpus Iuris Civilis, Vol. III, ed. stereotypa quinta, *Novellae,* quas recognovit Rudolfus Schoell, absolvit Guglielmus Kroll, Berolini: Apud Weidmannos, 1928.

Corpus Scriptorum Ecclesiasticorum Latinorum, Editum consilio et impensis Academiae Litterarum Caesareae Vindobonensis, Vindobonae: apud Geroldi Filium, 1866– .

Decretales D. Gregorii Papae IX una cum Glossis Restitutae, Romae, 1582.

Decretum Francisci Gratiani emendatum et notitionibus illustratum una cum Glossis Gregorii XIII, Pont. Max., iussu editum, 2 vols., Romae, 1852.

Institutionum ad Oblatos S. Ambrosii Pertinentium Epitome, Mediolani: apud Dominicum Bellagatam, 1716.

Jaffé, Philippus, *Regesta Pontificum Romanorum ab condita Ecclesia ad annum post Christum natum MCXCVIII,* ed. 2. correctam et auctam auspiciis Gulielmi Wattenbach curaverunt S. Loewenfeld, F. Kaltenbrunner, P. Ewald, 2 vols. in 1, Lipsiae, 1885–1888.

Mansi, J. D., *Sacrorum Conciliorum Nova et Amplissima Collectio,* 53 vols. in 60, Paris, Leipzig, Arnhem, 1901-1927.

Normae secundum quas Sacra Congregatio Episcoporum et Regularium procedere solet in Approbandis Novis Institutis votorum simplicium, Romae: Typis S. C. de Propaganda Fide, 1901.

Pallottini, Salvator, *Collectio omnium conclusionum et resolutionum quae in causis propositis apud Sacram Congregationem Cardinalium S. Concilii Tridentini Interpretum prodierunt ab eius institutione, anno MDLXXIX ad MDCCCLX, distinctis titulis alphabetico ordine per materias digesta,* 18 vols., Romae, 1868–1895.

Potthast, Augustus, *Regesta Pontificum Romanorum, inde ab anno post Christum natum MCXCVIII ad annum MCCCIV,* 2 vols., Berolini, 1874–1875.

Regula et Constitutiones Congregationis Missionis a Pretioso Sanguine D. N. J. C., Carthagena, Ohio, 1946.

Schema Constitutionum Congregationis a Missione approbationi Conventus Generalis XXXI subjiciendum, Lutetiae Parisiorum, 1947.

Schroeder, H. J., *Canons and Decrees of the Council of Trent, Text Translation and Commentary,* St. Louis-London: B. Herder & Co., 1941.

REFERENCE WORKS

Augustine, Charles, *A Commentary on the New Code of Canon Law,* 8 vols., Vol. III, St. Louis: Herder & Co., 1919.

Ayrinhac, H. A., *Penal Legislation in the New Code of Canon Law,* New York: Benziger Bros., 1936.

Bachofen, Augustinus, *Compendium Juris Regularium,* Neo-Eboraci: Benziger Bros., 1903.

Bakalarczyk, Richardus, *De Novitiatu,* The Catholic University of America Canon Law Studies, n. 36, Washington, D. C.: The Catholic University of America, 1927.

Balzer, Ralph F., *The Computation of Time in a Canonical Novitiate,* The Catholic University of America Canon Law Studies, n. 212, Washington, D. C.: The Catholic University of America Press, 1945.

Bastien, Pierre, *Directoire Canonique à l'Usage des Congrégations à Voeux Simples,* 3. ed., Bruges: Charles Beyaert, 1923.

Berutti, Christophorus, *Institutiones Iuris Canonici,* 6 vols., Vol. III, *De Religiosis,* Taurini-Romae: Marietti, 1936.

Beste, Udalricus, *Introductio in Codicem,* 2. ed., Collegeville, Minnesota; St. John's Abbey Press, 1944.

Biederlack, J.—Führich, M., *De Religiosis,* 2. ed., Oeniponte: Rauch, 1919.

Bouix, Dominicus, *Tractatus de Jure Regularium,* 2 vols., Parisiis, 1857.

Bouscaren, T. L.—Ellis, A. C., *Canon Law, A Text and Commentary,* Milwaukee: Bruce, 1946.

Butler, Cuthbert, *Benedictine Monachism,* London: Longmans, Green and Co., 1919.

Cance, Adrien, *Le Code de Droit Canonique, Commentaire succinct et pratique,* 7. ed., 3 vols., Paris: Gabalda et Cie., 1946.

Cappello, Felix M., *Summa Iuris Canonici in Usum Scholarum Concinnata,* 3 vols., Vol. II, 4. ed., 1945; Vol. III, 2. ed., 1940, Romae: apud Aedes Universitatis Gregorianae.

Catholic Encyclopedia, The, 15 vols. with Index and 2 Supplements, New York, 1907-1922.

Cayré, F., *Manual of Patrology and History of Theology* (translated by H. Howitt), 2 vols., Tournai: Desclée & Co., 1936-1940.

Chelodi, Ioannes, *Ius Canonicum de Personis,* 3. ed. curavit Pius Ciprotti, Vicenza: Libreria Moderna Editrice, 1942.

Cocchi, Guidus, *Commentarium in Codicem Iuris Canonici ad Usum Scholarum,* 8 vols. in 5, Liber II, Pars II, *De Religiosis,* 3. ed., Taurinorum Augustae, 1932.

Coronata, Matthaeus Conte a, *Institutiones Iuris Canonici ad Usum Utriusque Cleri et Scholarum,* 2. ed., 5 vols., Taurini: Marietti, 1939-1945.

———, *Institutiones Iuris Canonici, De Sacramentis,* 3 vols., Taurini-Romae: Marietti, 1943-1946.

Coste, Pierre, *Monsieur Vincent,* 3 vols., Paris: Desclée, de Brouwer, 1931.

Creusen, J., *Religious Men and Women in the Code,* translated by Edward Garesché, 4 Eng. ed. by Adam Ellis, Milwaukee: Bruce, 1940.

Currier, Charles W., *History of Religious Orders,* New York, 1896.

Fagnanus, Prosper, *Commentarium in Quinque Libros Decretalium,* 4 vols., Venetiis, 1697.

Fanfani, Ludovicus, *De Iure Religiosorum ad Normam Codicis Iuris Canonici,* 2. ed., Taurini-Romae: Marietti, 1925.

George, André, *L'Oratoire,* Paris: Bernard Grasset, 1928.

Georges, Emile, *Saint Jean Eudes,* Paris: Letheilleux, 1936.

Goyeneche, S., *Iuris Canonici Summa Principia de Religiosis,* Romae: Tip. Pol. "Cuore di Maria," 1938.

Hermant, G., *Histoire de l'Établissement des Ordres Réligieux et des Congrégations Régulières de l'Église,* Rouen, 1697.

Ladeuze, Paulin, *Étude sur le Cénobitisme Pakhômien pendant le IVe siècle et la Première Moitié du Ve,* Louvain: Typ. J. Van Linthout, 1898.

Migne, J. P., *Encyclopedie Théologique,* 3 series, 168 vols., Parisiis, 1845–1855.

———, *Patrologiae Cursus Completus, Series Latina (MPL),* 221 vols., Parisiis, 1844–1864; *Series Graeca (MPG),* 161 vols., Parisiis, 1857–1866.

Molitor, Raphael, *Religiosi Juris Capita Selecta, Ratisbon:* Fr. Pustet, 1909.

Mothon, Joseph P., *Traité sur l'État Réligieux,* Paris: Desclée, de Brouwer & Cie., 1922.

Oesterle, Gerardus, *Praelectiones Iuris Canonici,* Romae: apud Collegium S. Anselmi, 1931.

Pejška, Iosephus, *Ius Canonicum Religiosorum,* 3. ed., Friburgi Brisgoviae: Herder & Co., 1927.

Pignatelli, Iacobus, *Consultationes Canonicae,* 11 toms. in 4 vols., Coloniae Allobrogum, 1790.

Pirhing, Ernricus, *Synopsis Pirhingiana seu SS. Canonum Doctrina ex fusioribus quinque libris Henrici Pirhing in Compendium Redacta,* Romae, 1849.

Pisani, P., *The Congregations of Priests from the Sixteenth to the Eighteenth Century* (translated by Mother Mary Reginald), St. Louis: B. Herder & Co., 1930.

Prümmer, Dominicus, *Manuale Iuris Canonici in Usum Scholarum,* 5. ed., Friburgi Brisgoviae: Herder & Co., 1927.

Ramstein, Matthew, *A Manual of Canon Law,* Hoboken, New Jersey: Terminal Printing and Publishing Co., 1947.

Raus, J. B., *Institutiones Canonicae,* 2. ed., Parisiis: Vitte, 1931.

Regatillo, E., *Institutiones Iuris Canonici,* 2 vols., Vol. I, 2. ed., 1946; Vol. II, 1942, Santander: Aldus.

Reiffenstuel, Anacletus, *Ius Canonicum Universum,* 5 vols., Parisiis, 1864–1870.

Schaefer, Timotheus, *De Religiosis ad Normam Codicis Iuris Canonici,* 3. ed., Romae: Typis Polyglottis Vaticanis, S. A. L. E. R., 1940.

Schmalzgrueber, Franciscus, *Ius Ecclesiasticum Universum,* 5 vols. in 12, Romae, 1843–1845.

Stacpoole-Kenny, Louise M., *Saint Charles Borromeo,* New York: Benziger Brothers, 1911.

Stanton, W. A., *De Societatibus sive Virorum sive Mulierum in communi viventium sine votis,* Halifaxiae: apud Custodiam Librariam Maioris Seminarii a Sanctissimo Corde B. M. V., 1936.

Suarez, Franciscus, *Opera Omnia,* 28 vols., Parisiis: ed. L. Vivès, 1856–1861.

Thomassinus, Ludovicus, *Vetus et Nova Ecclesiae Disciplina,* 10 vols., Magontiaci, 1787.

Vermeersch, A.—Creusen, J., *Epitome Iuris Canonici cum Commentariis ad Scholas et ad Usum Privatum,* 6. ed., 3 vols., Mechliniae-Romae: H. Dessain, 1937–1946.

Wernz, Franciscus, *Ius Decretalium ad Usum Praelectionum in Scholis Textus Canonici sive Iuris Decretalium,* 2. ed., 6 vols., Romae-Prati, 1906–1913.

Wernz, F.—Vidal, Petrus, *Ius Canonicum ad Codicis Normam Exactum,* 7 toms. in 8 vols., Romae: apud Aedes Universitatis Gregorianae, 1923–1938; Tom. III, *De Religiosis,* 1933.

ARTICLES

Anonymous, "Traité des Congrégations Séculiers," *Analecta Iuris Pontificii,* V (1861), 52–103.

Creusen, J., "Sociétés Réligieuses," *Ephemerides Theologicae Lovanienses,* XI (1934), 778–786.

Frison, Basil M., "Ex-seminarian and Novice: A Clarification," *The Jurist,* VI (1946), 416–418.

Goyeneche, S., "Studia Canonica" ("De egressu e religione"), *CpR,* V (1924), 335–341.

Jombart, É., "Consultations" ("Profession Retardée par la Maladie"), *Revue des Communautés Réligieuses,* V (1929), 76–77.

Larraona, Arcadius, "Consultationes," *CpR,* I (1920), 180–181, 367–368; *CpRM,* XVI (1935), 430; XVII (1936), 9.

———, "Commentarium Codicis," *CpRM,* XVIII (1937), 319–326.

Steiger, R. P., "De propagatione et diffusione vitae religiosae," *Periodica de Re Canonica et Morali utilia praesertim Religiosis et Missionariis,* XIII (1924), (29)-(60); (73)-(100); (153)-(180).

Vermeersch, A., "Quaestiones de Codice Canonico," *Periodica,* IX (1921), (1)-(34).

Voltas, Petrus, "Consultationes," *CpR,* II (1921), 221, 368–370.

———, "Quaestio Canonica" ("De Novitiatus Interruptione"), *CpR,* II (1921), 76–85.

PERIODICALS

Analecta Iuris Pontificii, Romae, 1855–1869; Parisiis, 1872–1891.

Commentarium pro Religiosis, Romae, 1920–1934: ab anno 1935: *Commentarium pro Religiosis et Missionariis.*

Ephemerides Theologicae Lovanienses, Brugis: Beyaert, 1924– .

Jurist, The, Washington, D. C.: The Catholic University of America, 1941– .

Periodica de Religiosis et Missionariis, 8 vols., Brugis, 1905–1919; from 1920: *Periodica de Re Canonica et Morali utilia praesertim Religiosis et Missionariis,* 7 vols., Brugis, 1920–1927; from 1927: *Periodica de Re Morali, Canonica, Liturgica,* Brugis (1927–1936) et Romae (1937–).

Revue des Communautés Réligieuses, Louvain: Museum Lessianum, 1925- .

ABBREVIATIONS

AAS—*Acta Apostolicae Sedis.*

Analecta—*Analecta Iuris Pontificii.*

ASS—*Acta Sanctae Sedis.*

Bizzarri—*Collectanea in Usum Secretariae Sacrae Congregationis Episcoporum et Regularium.*

Bull. Rom. Taur.—*Bullarium Romanum, ed. Taurinensis.*

CLD—*The Canon Law Digest.*

Collectio—*Concilii Tridentini Diariorum, Actorum, Epistularum Tractatuum, Nova Collectio.*

CpR—*Commentarium pro Religiosis.*

CpRM—*Commentarium pro Religiosis et Missionariis.*

CSEL—*Corpus Scriptorum Ecclesiasticorum Latinorum.*

Fontes—*Codicis Iuris Canonici Fontes,* cura . . . Gasparri editi.

Mansi—*Sacrorum Conciliorum Nova et Amplissima Collectio.*

MPG—Migne, *Patrologia Graeca.*

MPL—Migne, *Patrologia Latina.*

Pallottini—*Collectio omnium conclusionum et resolutionum quae in causis propositis apud Sacram Congregationem Cardinalium S. Concilii Tridentini Interpretum prodierunt ab eius institutione, anno MDLXXIX ad MDCCCLX, distinctis titulis alphabetico ordine per materias digesta.*

Periodica—*Periodica de Re Morali, Canonica, Liturgica.*

Pont. Comm. ad Cod. Interpr.—Pontificia Commissio ad Codicis canones authentice interpretandos.

BIOGRAPHICAL NOTE

Joseph Louis Waters was born on May 24, 1920, in Philadelphia, Pennsylvania. He received his elementary education at Our Lady of Lourdes School in that city, and attended the West Philadelphia Catholic High School for Boys, from which he graduated in 1936. He then entered Epiphany Apostolic College at Newburgh, New York, finishing his course of studies in 1938. In that same year he was admitted to the Josephite novitiate and was professed as a member of the Society of Saint Joseph of the Sacred Heart on July 16, 1939. He completed the courses in Philosophy and Theology at Saint Joseph's Seminary, Washington, D. C., and was ordained to the priesthood on February 3, 1945. Following a period of parochial work at Holy Redeemer Church, Washington, D. C., he enrolled in the School of Canon Law of the Catholic University of America in October, 1946. He received the degree of the Baccalaureate in Canon Law in June, 1947, and the degree of the Licentiate in Canon Law in June, 1948.

INDEX

Canon Law Studies *

1. Freriks, Rev. Celestine A., C.PP.S., J.C.D., Religious Congregations in Their External Relations, 121 pp., 1916.
2. Galliher, Rev. Daniel M., O.P., J.C.D., Canonical Elections, 117 pp., 1917.
3. Borkowski, Rev. Aurelius L., O.F.M., J.C.D., De Confraternitatibus Ecclesiasticis, 136 pp., 1918.
4. Castillo, Rev. Cayo, J.C.D., Disertacion Historico-Canonica sobre la Potestad del Cabildo en Sede Vacante o Impedida del Vicario Capitular, 99 pp., 1919 (1918).
5. Kubelbeck, Rev. William J., S.T.B., J.C.D., The Sacred Penitentiaria and Its Relation to Faculties of Ordinaries and Priests, 129 pp., 1918.
6. Petrovits, Rev. Joseph J. C., S.T.D., J.C.D., The New Church Law on Matrimony, X-461 pp., 1919.
7. Hickey, Rev. John J., S.T.B., J.C.D., Irregularities and Simple Impediments in the New Code of Canon Law, 100 pp., 1920.
8. Klekotka, Rev. Peter J., S.T.B., J.C.D., Diocesan Consultors, 179 pp., 1920.
9. Wanenmacher, Rev. Francis, J.C.D., The Evidence in Ecclesiastical Procedure Affecting the Marriage Bond, 1920 (Printed 1935).
10. Golden, Rev. Henry Francis, J.C.D., Parochial Benefices in the New Code, IV-119 pp., 1921 (Printed 1925).
11. Koudelka, Rev. Charles J., J.C.D., Pastors, Their Rights and Duties According to the New Code of Canon Law, 211 pp., 1921.
12. Melo, Rev. Antonius, O.F.M., J.C.D., De Exemptione Regularium, X-188 pp., 1921.
13. Schaaf, Rev. Valentine Theodore, O.F.M., S.T.B., J.C.D., The Cloister, X-180 pp., 1921.
14. Burke, Rev. Thomas Joseph, S.T.D., J.C.D., Competence in Ecclesiastical Tribunals, IV-117 pp., 1922.
15. Leech, Rev. George Leo, J.C.D., A Comparative Study of the Constitution "Apostolicae Sedis" and the "Codex Juris Canonici," 179 pp., 1922.
16. Motry, Rev. Hubert Louis, S.T.D., J.C.D., Diocesan Faculties According to the Code of Canon Law, II-167 pp., 1922.
17. Murphy, Rev. George Lawrence, J.C.D., Delinquencies and Penalties in the Administration and the Reception of the Sacraments, IV-121 pp., 1923.

* All published numbers are available from the Catholic University of America Press, 621 Michigan Ave., N.E., Washington 17, D. C., except the following numbers: 1-114 inclusive, and numbers 116, 118, 120, 122, 123, 162 and 198.

18. O'REILLY, REV. JOHN ANTHONY, S.T.B., J.C.D., Ecclesiastical Sepulture in the New Code of Canon Law, II-129 pp., 1923.
19. MICHALICKA, REV. WENCESLAS CYRILL, O.S.B., J.C.D., Judicial Procedure in Dismissal of Clerical Exempt Religious, 107 pp., 1923.
20. DARGIN, REV. EDWARD VINCENT, S.T.B., J.C.D., Reserved Cases According to the Code of Canon Law, IV-103 pp., 1924.
21. GODFREY, REV. JOHN A., S.T.B., J.C.D., The Right of Patronage According to the Code of Canon Law, 153 pp., 1924.
22. HAGEDORN, REV. FRANCIS EDWARD, J.C.D., General Legislation on Indulgences, II-154 pp., 1924.
23. KING, REV. JAMES IGNATIUS, J.C.D., The Administration of the Sacraments to Dying Non-Catholics, V-141 pp., 1924.
24. WINSLOW, REV. FRANCIS JOSEPH, M.M., J.C.D., Vicars and Prefects Apostolic, IV-149 pp., 1924.
25. CORREA, REV. JOSE SERVELION, S.T.L., J.C.D., La Potestad Legislativa de la Iglesia Catolica, IV-127 pp., 1925.
26. DUGAN, REV. HENRY FRANCIS, A.M., J.C.D., The Judiciary Department of the Diocesan Curia, 87 pp., 1925.
27. KELLER, REV. CHARLES FREDERICK, S.T.B., J.C.D., Mass Stipends, 167 pp., 1925.
28. PASCHANG, REV. JOHN LINUS, J.C.D., The Sacramentals According to the Code of Canon Law, 129 pp., 1925.
29. PIONTEK, REV. CYRILLUS, O.F.M., S.T.B., J.C.D., De Indulto Exclaustrationis necnon Saecularizationis, XIII-289 pp., 1925.
30. KEARNEY, REV. RICHARD JOSEPH, S.T.B., J.C.D., Sponsors at Baptism According to the Code of Canon Law, IV-127 pp., 1925.
31. BARTLETT, REV. CHESTER JOSEPH, A.M., LL.B., J.C.D., The Tenure of Parochial Property in the United States of America, V-108 pp., 1926.
32. KILKER, REV. ADRIAN JEROME, J.C.D., Extreme Unction, V-425 pp., 1926.
33. McCORMICK, REV. ROBERT EMMETT, J.C.D., Confessors of Religious, VIII-266 pp., 1926.
34. MILLER, REV. NEWTON THOMAS, J.C.D., Founded Masses According to the Code of Canon Law, VII-93 pp., 1926.
35. ROELKER, REV. EDWARD G., S.T.D., J.C.D., Principles of Privilege According to the Code of Canon Law, XI-166 pp., 1926.
36. BAKALARCZYK, REV. RICHARDUS, M.I.C., J.U.D., De Novitiatu, VIII-208 pp., 1927.
37. PIZZUTI, REV. LAWRENCE, O.F.M., J.U.L., De Parochis Religiosis, 1927. (Not Printed.)
38. BLILEY, REV. NICHOLAS MARTIN, O.S.B., J.C.D., Altars According to the Code of Canon Law, XIX-132 pp., 1927.
39. BROWN, MR. BRENDAN FRANCIS, A.B., LL.M., J.U.D., The Canonical Juristic Personality with Special Reference to its Status in the United States of America, V-212 pp., 1927.

40. Cavanaugh, Rev. William Thomas, C.P., J.U.D., The Reservation of the Blessed Sacrament, VIII-101 pp., 1927.
41. Doheny, Rev. William J., C.S.C., A.B., J.U.D., Church Property: Modes of Acquisition, X-118 pp., 1927.
42. Feldhaus, Rev. Aloysius H., C.PP.S., J.C.D., Oratories, IX-141 pp., 1927.
43. Kelly, Rev. James Patrick, A.B., J.C.D., The Jurisdiction of the Simple Confessor, X-208 pp., 1927.
44. Neuberger, Rev. Nicholas J., J.C.D., Canon 6 or the Relation of the Codex Juris Canonici to the Preceding Legislation, V-95 pp., 1927.
45. O'Keefe, Rev. Gerald Michael, J.C.D., Matrimonial Dispensations, Powers of Bishops, Priests, and Confessors, VIII-232 pp., 1927.
46. Quigley, Rev. Joseph A. M., A.B., J.C.D., Condemned Societies, 139 pp., 1927.
47. Zaplotnik, Rev. Johannes Leo, J.C.D., De Vicariis Foraneis, X-142 pp., 1927.
48. Duskie, Rev. John Aloysius, A.B., J.C.D., The Canonical Status of the Orientals in the United States, VIII-196 pp., 1928.
49. Hyland, Rev. Francis Edward, J.C.D., Excommunication, Its Nature, Historical Development and Effects, VIII-181 pp., 1928.
50. Reinmann, Rev. Gerald Joseph, O.M.C., J.C.D., The Third Order Secular of Saint Francis, 201 pp., 1928.
51. Schenk, Rev. Francis J., J.C.D., The Matrimonial Impediments of Mixed Religion and Disparity of Cult, XVI-318 pp., 1929.
52. Coady, Rev. John Joseph, S.T.D., J.U.D., A.M., The Appointment of Pastors, VIII-150 pp., 1929.
53. Kay, Rev. Thomas Henry, J.C.D., Competence in Matrimonial Procedure, VIII-164 pp., 1929.
54. Turner, Rev. Sidney Joseph, C.P., J.U.D., The Vow of Poverty, XLIX-217 pp., 1929.
55. Kearney, Rev. Raymond A., A.B., S.T.D., J.C.D., The Principles of Delegation, VII-149 pp., 1929.
56. Conran, Rev. Edward James, A.B., J.C.D., The Interdict, V-163 pp., 1930.
57. O'Neill, Rev. William H., J.C.D., Papal Rescripts of Favor, VII-218 pp., 1930.
58. Bastnagel, Rev. Clement Vincent, J.U.D., The Appointment of Parochial Adjutants and Assistants, XV-257 pp., 1930.
59. Ferry, Rev. William A., A.B., J.C.D., Stole Fees, V-136 pp., 1930.
60. Costello, Rev. John Michael, A.B., J.C.D., Domicile and Quasi-Domicile, VII-201 pp., 1930.
61. Kremer, Rev. Michael Nicholas, A.B., S.T.B., J.C.D., Church Support in the United States, VI-136 pp., 1930.
62. Angulo, Rev. Luis, C.M., J.C.D., Legislation de la Iglesia sobre la intencion en la application de la Santa Misa, VII-104 pp., 1931.

63. Frey, Rev. Wolfgang Norbert, O.S.B., A.B., J.C.D., The Act of Religious Profession, VIII-174 pp., 1931.
64. Roberts, Rev. James Brendan, A.B., J.C.D., The Banns of Marriage, XIV-140 pp., 1931.
65. Ryder, Rev. Raymond Aloysius, A.B., J.C.D., Simony, IX-151 pp., 1931.
66. Campagna, Rev. Angelo, Ph.D., J.U.D., Il Vicario Generale del Vescovo, VII-205 pp., 1931.
67. Cox, Rev. Joseph Godfrey, A.B., J.C.D., The Administration of Seminaries, VI-124 pp., 1931.
68. Gregory, Rev. Donald J., J.U.D., The Pauline Privilege, XV-165 pp., 1931.
69. Donohue, Rev. John F., J.C.D., The Impediment of Crime, VII-110 pp., 1931.
70. Dooley, Rev. Eugene A., O.M.I., J.C.D., Church Law on Sacred Relics, IX-143 pp., 1931.
71. Orth, Rev. Clement Raymond, O.M.C., J.C.D., The Approbation of Religious Institutes, 171 pp., 1931.
72. Pernicone, Rev. Joseph M., A.B., J.C.D., The Ecclesiastical Prohibition of Books, XII-267 pp., 1932.
73. Clinton, Rev. Connell, A.B., J.C.D., The Paschal Precept, IX-108 pp., 1932.
74. Donnelly, Rev. Francis B., A.M., S.T.L., J.C.D., The Diocesan Synod, VIII-125 pp., 1932.
75. Torrente, Rev. Camilo, C.M.F., J.C.D., Las Procesiones Sagradas, V-145 pp., 1932.
76. Murphy, Rev. Edwin J., C.PP.S., J.C.D., Suspension Ex Informata Conscientia, XI-122 pp., 1932.
77. MacKenzie, Rev. Eric F., A.M., S.T.L., J.C.D., The Delict of Heresy in its Commission, Penalization, Absolution, VII-124 pp., 1932.
78. Lyons, Rev. Avitus E., S.T.B., J.C.D., The Collegiate Tribunal of First Instance, XI-147 pp., 1932.
79. Connolly, Rev. Thomas A., J.C.D., Appeals, XI-195 pp., 1932.
80. Sangmeister, Rev. Joseph V., A.B., J.C.D., Force and Fear as Precluding Matrimonial Consent, V-211 pp., 1932.
81. Jaeger, Rev. Leo A., A.B., J.C.D., The Administration of Vacant and Quasi-Vacant Episcopal Sees in the United States, IX-229 pp., 1932.
82. Rimlinger, Rev. Herbert T., J.C.D., Error Invalidating Matrimonial Consent, VII-79 pp., 1932.
83. Barrett, Rev. John D. M., S.S., J.C.D., A Comparative Study of the Third Plenary Council of Baltimore and the Code, IX-221 pp., 1932.
84. Carberry, Rev. John J., Ph.D., S.T.D., J.C.D., The Juridical Form of Marriage, X-177 pp., 1934.
85. Dolan, Rev. John L., A.B., J.C.D., The Defensor Vinculi, XII-157 pp., 1934.

86. HANNAN, REV. JEROME D., A.M., S.T.D., LL.B., J.C.D., The Canon Law of Wills, IX-517 pp., 1934.
87. LEMIEUX, REV. DELISE A., A.M., J.C.D., The Sentence in Ecclesiastical Procedure, IX-131 pp., 1934.
88. O'ROURKE, REV. JAMES J., A.B., J.C.D., Parish Registers, VII-109 pp., 1934.
89. TIMLIN, REV. BARTHOLOMEW, O.F.M., A.M., J.C.D., Conditional Matrimonial Consent, X-381 pp., 1934.
90. WAHL, REV. FRANCIS X., A.B., J.C.D., The Matrimonial Impediments of Consanguinity and Affinity, VI-125 pp., 1934.
91. WHITE, REV. ROBERT J., A.B., LL.B., S.T.B., J.C.D., Canonical Ante-Nuptial Promises and the Civil Law, VI-152 pp., 1934.
92. HERRERA, REV. ANTONIO PARRA, O.C.D., J.C.D., Legislacion Ecclesiastica sobra el Ayuno y la Abstinencia, XI-191 pp., 1935.
93. KENNEDY, REV. EDWIN J., J.C.D., The Special Matrimonial Process in Cases of Evident Nullity, X-165 pp., 1935.
94. MANNING, REV. JOHN J., A.B., J.C.D., Presumption of Law in Matrimonial Procedure, XI-111 pp., 1935.
95. MOEDER, REV. JOHN M., J.C.D., The Proper Bishop for Ordination and Dimissorial Letters, VII-135 pp., 1935.
96. O'MARA, REV. WILLIAM A., A.B., J.C.D., Canonical Causes for Matrimonial Dispensations, IX-155 pp., 1935.
97. REILLY, REV. PETER, J.C.D., Residence of Pastors, IX-81 pp., 1935.
98. SMITH, REV. MARINER T., O.P., S.T.Lr., J.C.D., The Penal Law for Religious, VII-169 pp., 1935.
99. WHALEN, REV. DONALD W., A.M., J.C.D., The Value of Testimonial Evidence in Matrimonial Procedure, XIII-297 pp., 1935.
100. CLEARY, REV. JOSEPH F., J.C.D., Canonical Limitations on the Alienation of Church Property, VIII-141 pp., 1936.
101. GLYNN, REV. JOHN C., J.C.D., The Promoter of Justice, XX-337 pp., 1936.
102. BRENNAN, REV. JAMES H., S.S., M.A., S.T.B., J.C.D., The Simple Convalidation of Marriage, VI-135 pp., 1937.
103. BRUNINI, REV. JOSEPH BERNARD, J.C.D., The Clerical Obligations of Canons 139 and 142, X-121 pp., 1937.
104. CONNOR, REV. MAURICE, A.B., J.C.D., The Administrative Removal of Pastors, VIII-159 pp., 1937.
105. GUILFOYLE, REV. MERLIN JOSEPH, J.C.D., Custom, XI-144 pp., 1937.
106. HUGHES, REV. JAMES AUSTIN, A.B., A.M., J.C.D., Witnesses in Criminal Trials of Clerics, IX-140 pp., 1937.
107. JANSEN, REV. RAYMOND J., A.B., S.T.L., J.C.D., Canonical Provisions for Catechetical Instruction, VII-153 pp., 1937.
108. KEALY, REV. JOHN JAMES, A.B., J.C.D., The Introductory Libellus in Church Court Procedure, XI-121 pp., 1937.

109. McManus, Rev. James Edward, C.SS.R., J.C.D., The Administration of Temporal Goods in Religious Institutes, XVI-196 pp., 1937.
110. Moriarty, Rev. Eugene James, J.C.D., Oaths in Ecclesiastical Courts, X-115 pp., 1937.
111. Rainer, Rev. Eligius George, C.SS.R., J.C.D., Suspension of Clerics, XVII-249 pp., 1937.
112. Reilly, Rev. Thomas F., C.SS.R., J.C.D., Visitation of Religious, VI-195 pp., 1938.
113. Moriarity, Rev. Francis E., C.SS.R., J.C.D., The Extraordinary Absolution from Censures, XV-334 pp., 1938.
114. Connolly, Rev. Nicholas P., J.C.D., The Canonical Erection of Parishes, X-132 pp., 1938.
115. Donovan, Rev. James Joseph, J.C.D., The Pastor's Obligation in Prenuptial Investigation, XII-322 pp., 1938.
116. Harrigan, Rev. Robert J., M.A., S.T.B., J.C.D., The Radical Sanation of Invalid Marriages, VIII-208 pp., 1938.
117. Boffa, Rev. Conrad Humbert, J.C.D., Canonical Provisions for Catholic Schools, VII-211 pp., 1939.
118. Parsons, Rev. Anscar John, O.M.Cap., J.C.D., Canonical Elections, XII-236 pp., 1939.
119. Reilly, Rev. Edward Michael, A.B., J.C.D., The General Norms of Dispensation, XII-156 pp., 1939.
120. Ryan, Rev. Gerald Aloysius, A.B., J.C.D., Principles of Episcopal Jurisdiction, XII-172 pp., 1939.
121. Burton, Rev. Francis James, C.S.C., A.B., J.C.D., A Commentary on Canon 1125, X-222 pp., 1940.
122. Miaskiewicz, Rev. Francis Sigismund, J.C.D., Supplied Jurisdiction According to Canon 209, XII-340 pp., 1940.
123. Rice, Rev. Patrick William, A.B., J.C.D., Proof of Death in Prenuptial Investigation, VIII-156 pp., 1940.
124. Anglin, Rev. Thomas Francis, M.S., J.C.D., The Eucharistic Fast, VIII-183 pp., 1941.
125. Coleman, Rev. John Jerome, J.C.D., The Minister of Confirmation, VI-153 pp., 1941.
126. Downs, Rev. John Emmanuel, A.B., J.C.D., The Concept of Clerical Immunity, XI-163 pp., 1941.
127. Esswein, Rev. Anthony Albert, J.C.D., Extrajudicial Penal Powers of Ecclesiastical Superiors, X-144 pp., 1941.
128. Farrell, Rev. Benjamin Francis, M.A., S.T.L., J.C.D., The Rights and Duties of the Local Ordinary Regarding Congregations of Women Religious of Pontifical Approval, V-195 pp., 1941.
129. Feeney, Rev. Thomas John, A.B., S.T.L., J.C.D., Restitutio in Integrum, VI-169 pp., 1941.
130. Findlay, Rev. Stephen William, O.S.B., A.B., J.C.D., Canonical

Norms Governing the Deposition and Degradation of Clerics, XVII-279 pp., 1941.

131. GOODWINE, REV. JOHN, A.B., S.T.L., J.C.D., The Right of the Church to Acquire Property, VIII-119 pp., 1941.

132. HESTON, REV. EDWARD LOUIS, C.S.C., Ph.D., S.T.D., J.C.D., The Alienation of Church Property in the United States, XII-222 pp., 1941.

133. HOGAN, REV. JAMES JOHN, A.B., S.T.L., J.C.D., Judicial Advocates and Procurators, XIII-200 pp., 1941.

134. KEALY, REV. THOMAS M., A.B., Litt.B., J.C.D., Dowry of Women Religious, IX-152 pp., 1941.

135. KEENE, REV. MICHAEL JAMES, O.S.B., J.C.D., Religious Ordinaries and Canon 198, V-164 pp., 1942.

136. KERIN, REV. CHARLES A., S.S., M.A., S.T.B., J.C.D., The Privation of Christian Burial, XVI-279 pp., 1941.

137. LOUIS, REV. WILLIAM FRANCIS, M.A., J.C.D., Diocesan Archives, X-101 pp., 1941.

138. McDEVITT, REV. GILBERT JOSEPH, A.B., J.C.D., Legitimacy and Legitimation, X-247 pp., 1941.

139. McDONOUGH, REV. THOMAS JOSEPH, A.B., J.C.D., Apostolic Administrators, X-217 pp., 1941.

140. MEIER, REV. CARL ANTHONY, A.B., J.C.D., Penal Administrative Procedure Against Negligent Pastors, XI-240 pp., 1941.

141. SCHMIDT, REV. JOHN ROGG, A.B., J.C.D., The Principles of Authentic Interpretation in Canon 17 of the Code of Canon Law, XII-331 pp., 1941.

142. SLAFKOSKY, REV. ANDREW LEONARD, A.B., J.C.D., The Canonical Episcopal Visitation of the Diocese, X-197 pp., 1941.

143. SWABODA, REV. INNOCENT ROBERT, O.F.M., J.C.D., Ignorance in Relation to the Imputability of Delicts, IX-271 pp., 1941.

144. DUBÉ, REV. ARTHUR JOSEPH, A. B., J.C.D., The General Principles for the Reckoning of Time in Canon Law, VIII-299 pp., 1941.

145. McBRIDE, REV. JAMES T., A.B., J.C.D., Incardination and Excardination of Seculars, XX-585 pp., 1941.

146 KRÓL, REV. JOHN T., J.C.D., The Defendant in Ecclesiastical Trials, XII-207 pp., 1942.

147. COMYNS, REV. JOSEPH J., C.SS.R., A.B., J.C.D., Papal and Episcopal Administration of Church Property, XIV-155 pp., 1942.

148. BARRY, REV. GARRETT FRANCIS, O.M.I., J.C.D., Violation of the Cloister, XII-260 pp., 1942.

149. BOLDUC, REV. GATIEN, C.S.V., A.B., S.T.L., J.C.D., Les Études dans les Religions Cléricales, VIII-155 pp., 1942.

150. BOYLE, REV. DAVID JOHN, M.A., J.C.D., The Juridic Effects of Moral Certitude on Pre-Nuptial Guarantees, XII-188 pp., 1942.

151. CANAVAN, REV. WALTER JOSEPH, M.A., Litt.D., J.C.D., The Profession of Faith, XII-143 pp., 1942.

152. Desrochers, Rev. Bruno, A.B., Ph.L., S.T.B., J.C.D., Le Premier Concile Plénier de Québéc et le Code de Droit Canonique, XIV-186 pp., 1942.
153. Dillon, Rev. Robert Edward, A.B., J.C.D., Common Law Marriage, X-148 pp., 1942.
154. Dodwell, Rev. Edward John, Ph.D., S.T.B., J.C.D., The Time and Place for the Celebration of Marriage, X-156 pp., 1942.
155. Donnellan, Rev. Thomas Andrew, A.B., J.C.D., The Obligation of the Missa pro Populo, VII-131 pp., 1942.
156. Eltz, Rev. Louis Anthony, A.B., J.C.D., Cooperation in Crime, XII-208 pp., 1942.
157. Gass, Rev. Sylvester Francis, M.A., J.C.D., Ecclesiastical Pensions, XI-206 pp., 1942.
158. Guiniven, Rev. John Joseph, C.SS.R., J.C.D., The Precept of Hearing Mass, XIV-188 pp., 1942.
159. Gluczynski, Rev. John Theophilus, J.C.D., The Desecration and Violation of Churches, X-126 pp., 1942.
160. Hammill, Rev. John Leo, M.A., J.C.D., The Obligations of the Traveler According to Canon 14, VIII-204 pp., 1942.
161. Haydt, Rev. John Joseph, A.B., J.C.D., Reserved Benefices, XI-148 pp., 1942.
162. Huser, Rev. Roger John, O.F.M., A.B., J.C.D., The Crime of Abortion in Canon Law, XII-187 pp., 1942.
163. Kearney, Rev. Francis Patrick, A.B., S.T.L., J.C.D., The Principles of Canon 1127, X-162 pp., 1942.
164. Linahen, Rev. Leo James, S.T.L., J.C.D., De Absolutione Complicis In Peccato Turpi, 114 pp., 1942.
165. McCloskey, Rev. Joseph Aloysius, A.B., J.C.D., The Subject of Ecclesiastical Law According to Canon 12, XVII-246 pp., 1942.
166. O'Neill, Rev. Francis Joseph, C.SS.R., J.C.D., The Dismissal of Religious in Temporary Vows, XIII-220 pp., 1942.
167. Prince, Rev. John Edward, A.B., S.T.B., J.C.D., The Diocesan Chancellor, X-136 pp., 1942.
168. Riesner, Rev. Albert Joseph, C.SS.R., J.C.D., Apostates and Fugitives from Religious Institutes, IX-168 pp., 1942.
169. Stenger, Rev. Joseph Bernard, J.C.D., The Mortgaging of Church Property, 186 pp., 1942.
170. Waldron, Rev. Joseph Francis, A.B., J.C.D., The Minister of Baptism, XII-197 pp., 1942.
171. Willett, Rev. Robert Albert, J.C.D., The Probative Value of Documents in Ecclesiastical Trials, X-124 pp., 1942.
172. Woeber, Rev. Edward Martin, M.A., J.C.D., The Interpellations, XII-161 pp., 1942.
173. Benko, Rev. Matthew Aloysius, O.S.B., M.A., J.C.D., The Abbot *Nullius*, XVI-148 pp., 1943.

174. CHRIST, REV. JOSEPH JAMES, M.A., S.T.L., J.C.D., Dispensation from Vindicative Penalties, XIV-285 pp., 1943.
175. CLANCY, REV. PATRICK M. J., O.P., A.B., S.T.Lr., J.C.D., The Local Religious Superior, X-229 pp., 1943.
176. CLARKE, REV. THOMAS JAMES, J.C.D., Parish Societies, XII-147 pp., 1943.
177. CONNOLLY, REV. JOHN PATRICK, S.T.L., J.C.D., Synodal Examiners and Parish Priest Consultors, X-223 pp., 1943.
178. DRUMM, REV. WILLIAM MARTIN, A.B., J.C.D., Hospital Chaplains, XII-175 pp., 1943.
179. FLANAGAN, REV. BERNARD JOSEPH, A.B., S.T.L., J.C.D., The Canonical Erection of Religious Houses, X-147 pp., 1943.
180. KELLEHER, REV. STEPHEN JOSEPH, A.B., S.T.B., J.C.D., Discussions with Non-Catholics: Canonical Legislation, X-93 pp., 1943.
181. LEWIS, REV. GORDIAN, C.P., J.C.D., Chapters in Religious Institutes, XII-169 pp., 1943.
182. MARX, REV. ADOLPH, J.C.D., The Declaration of Nullity of Marriages Contracted Outside the Church, X-151 pp., 1943.
183. MATULENAS, REV. RAYMOND ANTHONY, O.S.B., A.B., J.C.D., Communication, a Source of Privileges, XII-225 pp., 1943.
184. O'LEARY, REV. CHARLES GERARD, C.SS.R., J.C.D., Religious Dismissed After Perpetual Profession, X-213 pp., 1943.
185. POWER, REV. CORNELIUS MICHAEL, J.C.D., The Blessing of Cemeteries, XII-231 pp., 1943.
186. SHUHLER, REV. RALPH VINCENT, O.S.A., J.C.D., Privileges of Regulars to Absolve and Dispense, XII-195 pp., 1943.
187. ZIOLKOWSKI, REV. THADDEUS STANISLAUS, A.B., J.C.D., The Consecration and Blessing of Churches, XII-151 pp., 1943.
188. HENEGHAN, REV. JOHN JOSEPH, S.T.D., J.C.D., The Marriages of Unworthy Catholics: Canons 1065 and 1066, XVI-213 pp., 1944.
189. CARROLL, REV. COLEMAN FRANCIS, M.A., S.T.L., J.C.L., Charitable Institutions.
190. CIESLUK, REV. JOSEPH EDWARD, Ph.B., S.T.L., J.C.D., National Parishes in the United States, VI-178 pp., 1944.
191. COBURN, REV. VINCENT PAUL, A.B., J.C.D., Marriages of Conscience, XII-172 pp., 1944.
192. CONNORS, REV. CHARLES PAUL, C.S.Sp., A.B., J.C.D., Extra-Judicial Procurators in the Code of Canon Law, X-94 pp., 1944.
193. COYLE, REV. PAUL RAYMOND, A.B., J.C.D., Judicial Exceptions, X-142 pp., 1944.
194. FAIR, REV. BARTHOLOMEW FRANCIS, A.B., S.T.L., J.C.D., The Impediment of Abduction, XII-122 pp., 1944.
195. GALLAGHER, REV. THOMAS RAPHAEL, O.P., A.B., S.T.Lr., J.C.D., The Examination of the Qualities of the Ordinand, X-166 pp., 1944.
196. GANNON, REV. JOHN MARK, S.T.L., J.C.D., The Interstices Required for the Promotion to Orders, XII-100 pp., 1944.

197. Goldsmith, Rev. J. William, B.C.S., S.T.L., J.C.D., The Competence of Church and State over Marriage—Disputed Points, X-128 pp., 1944.
198. Goodwine, Rev. Joseph Gerard, A.B., S.T.D., J.C.D., The Reception of Converts, XIV-326 pp., 1944.
199. Kowalski, Rev. Romuald Eugene, O.F.M., A.B., J.C.D., Sustenance of Religious Houses of Regulars, X-174 pp., 1944.
200. McCoy, Rev. Alan Edward, O.F.M., J.C.D., Force and Fear in Relation to Delictual Imputability and Penal Responsibility, XII-160 pp., 1944.
201. McDevitt, Rev. Vincent John, Ph.B., S.T.L., J.C.L., Perjury.
202. Martin, Rev. Thomas Owen, Ph.D., S.T.D., J.C.D., Adverse Possession, Prescription and Limitation of Actions: The Canonical "Praescriptio," XX-208 pp., 1944.
203. Miklosovic, Rev. Paul John, A.B., J.C.L., Attempted Marriages and Their Consequent Juridic Effects.
204. Mundy, Rev. Thomas Maurice, A.B., S.T.L., J.C.D., The Union of Parishes, X—164 pp., 1944.
205. O'Dea, Rev. John Coyle, A.B., J.C.D., The Matrimonial Impediment of Nonage, VIII-126 pp., 1944.
206. Olalia, Rev. Alexander Ayson, S.T.L., J.C.D., A Comparative Study of the Christian Constitution of States and the Constitution of the Philippine Commonwealth, XII—136 pp., 1944.
207. Poisson, Rev. Pierre-Marie, C.S.C., A.B., Ph.L., Th.L., J.C.L., Droits Patrimoniaux des Maisons et des Églises Religieuses.
208. Stadalnikas, Rev. Casimir Joseph, M.I.C., J.C.D., Reservation of Censures, X-141 pp., 1944.
209. Sullivan, Rev. Eugene Henry, S.T.L., J.C.D., Proof of the Reception of the Sacraments, X—165 pp., 1944.
210. Vaughan, Rev. William Edward, J.C.D., Constitutions for Diocesan Courts, X-210 pp., 1944.
211. Paro, Rev. Gino, S.T.D., J.C.L., The Right of Apostolic Legation.
212. Balzer, Rev. Ralph Francis, C.P., J.C.D., The Computation of Time in a Canonical Novitiate, X—227 pp., 1945.
213. Dougherty, Rev. John Whelan, A.B., S.T.L., J.C.D., De Inquisitione Speciali, XII—195 pp., 1945.
214. Dziob, Rev. Michael Walter, J.C.D., The Sacred Congregation for the Oriental Church, XII—181 pp., 1945.
215. Eidenschink, Rev. John Albert, O.S.B., B.A., J.C.D, The Election of Bishops in the Letters of Pope Gregory the Great, VII—200 pp., 1945.
216. Gill, Rev. Nicholas, C.P., J.C.D., The Spiritual Prefect in Clerical Religious Houses of Study, X—140 pp., 1945.
217. Hynes, Rev. Harry Gerard, S.T.L., J.C.D., The Privileges of Cardinals, XII-183 pp., 1945.
218. McDevitt, Rev. Gerald Vincent, S.T.L., J.C.D., The Renunciation of an Ecclesiastical Office, XIV—179 pp., 1945.

219. Manning, Rev. Joseph Leroy, J.C.D., The Free Conferral of Offices, VIII—116 pp., 1945.
220. **Meyer, Rev. Louis G., O.S.B., A.B., S.T.B., J.C.D., Alms-Gathering** by Religious, XII—163 pp., 1945.
221. O'Donnell, Rev. Cletus Francis, M.A., J.C.D., The Marriage of Minors, XII—268 pp., 1945.
222. **Prunskis, Rev. Joseph, J.C.D., Comparative Law, Ecclesiastical and Civil, in Lithuanian Concordat, X—161 pp., 1945.**
223. **Sweeney, Rev. Francis Patrick, C.SS.R., J.C.D., The Reduction of Clerics to the Lay State, X—199 pp., 1945.**
224. Vogelpohl, Rev. Henry John, J.C.D., The Simple Impediments to Holy Orders, XVI—190 pp., 1945.
225. Brockhaus, Rev. Thomas Aquinas, O.S.B., A.B., J.C.D., Religious who Are Known as *Conversi*, X—127 pp., 1945.
226. Griese, Rev. N. Orville, S.T.D., J.C.D., The Marriage Contract and the Procreation of Offspring, XVI-224 pp., 1946.
227. Boudreaux, Rev. Warren Louis, J.C.D., The "*ab acatholicis nati*" of Canon 1099, § 2, XII-110 pp., 1946.
228. Bowe, Rev. Thomas Joseph, A.B., J.C.D., Religious Superioresses, VIII-206 pp., 1946.
229. Diederichs, Rev. Michael Ferdinand, S.C.J., J.C.D., The Jurisdiction of the Latin Ordinaries over their Oriental Subjects, XIV-153 pp., 1946.
230. Dingman, Rev. Maurice John, A.B., S.T.L., J.C.L., The Plaintiff in Contentious Trials.
231. Frison, Rev. Basil, C.M.F., M.Mus., J.C.D., The Retroactivity of Law, X-221 pp., 1946.
232. Galvin, Rev. William Anthony, M.A., J.C.D., The Administrative Transfer of Pastors, XII-288 pp., 1946.
233. Goracy, Rev. Joseph C., J.C.L., The Diriment Matrimonial Impediment of Major Orders.
234. Hale, Rev. Joseph Francis, M.A., S.T.L., J.C.L., The Pastor of Burial.
235. Henry, Rev. Joseph Arthur, A.B., J.C.D., The Mass and Holy Communion: Inter-Ritual Law, XII-138 pp., 1946.
236. Linenberger, Rev. Herbert, C.PP.S., J.C.L., The False Denunciation of an Innocent Confessor.
237. Lowry, Rev. James Martin, A.B., J.C.D., Dispensation from Private Vows, XII-266 pp., 1946.
238. Lynch, Rev. George Edward, A.B., S.T.L., J.C.D., Coadjutors and Auxiliaries of Bishops, X-107 pp., 1947.
239. Lynch, Rev. Timothy, M.S.SS.T., J.C.D., Contracts between Bishops and Religious Congregations, XIV-232 pp., 1946.
240. McClunn, Rev. Justin David, A.B., S.T.L., J.C.D., Administrative Recourse, VII-142 pp., 1946.

241. Lohmuller, Rev. Martin Nicholas, A.B., J.C.D., The Promulgation of Law, XII-140 pp., 1947.
242. McGrath, Rev. James, A.B., J.C.D., The Privilege of the Canon, XII-156 pp., 1946.
243. Marbach, Rev. Joseph Francis, A.B., J.C.D., Marriage Legislation for the Catholics of the Oriental Rites in the United States and Canada, XIV-314 pp., 1946.
244. Shimkus, Rev. Bernard Aloysius, A.B., J.C.L., The Determination and Transfer of Rite.
245. Smith, Rev. Vincent Michael, A.B., S.T.L., J.C.L., Ignorance Affecting Matrimonial Consent.
246. Wachtrle, Rev. Paul Anthony, A.B., J.C.L., The Baptism of the Children of Non-Catholics.
247. Crotty, Rev. Matthew Michael, J.C.D., The Recipient of First Holy Communion, X-142 pp., 1947.
248. Eagleton, Rev. George, J.C.L., The Quinquennial Faculties, Formula IV.
249. Gibbons, Rev. Marion Leo, C.M., J.C.D., Domicile of the Wife Unlawfully Separated from Her Husband, XIV-171 pp., 1947.
250. Kelly, Rev. Bernard Matthew, S.T.L., J.C.D., The Functions Reserved to Pastors, X-150 pp., 1947.
251. Kilcullen, Rev. Thomas John, LL.M., J.C.D., The Collegiate Moral Person as Party Litigant, X-150 pp., 1947.
252. Lafontaine, Rev. Germain Joseph, W.F., J.C.L., Relations Canoniques entre le Missionaire et Ses Superieurs.
253. Lane, Rev. Loras Thomas, J.C.L., Matrimonial Procedure in Ordinary Court of Second Instance.
254. Lover, Rev. James Francis, C.Ss.R., J.C.D., The Master of Novices, X-168 pp., 1947.
255. McNicholas, Rev. Timothy Joseph, J.C.D., The *Septimae Manus* Witness, XII—133 pp., 1947 (printed 1949).
256. Marositz, Rev. Joseph John, M.S.C., J.C.D., Obligations and Privileges of Religious Promoted to the Episcopal or Cardinalitial Dignities, XII-180 pp. 1947.
257. Murphy, Rev. Francis Joseph, J.C.D., Legislative Powers of the Provincial Council, XII-158 pp., 1947.
258. O'Brien, Rev. Romaeus William, O.Carm., J.C.D., The Provincial Superior in Religious Orders of Men, X-294 pp., 1947.
259. Pfaller, Rev. Benedict Anthony, O.S.B., J.C.L., *The ipso facto* Effected Dismissal of Religious.
260. Popek, Rev. Alphonse Sylvester, J.C.D., The Rights and Obligations of Metropolitans, XVIII-460 pp., 1947.
261. Ristuccia, Rev. Bernard Joseph, C.M., J.C.L., Quasi-Religious.
262. Sonntag, Rev. Nathaniel Louis, O.F.M.Cap., J.C.D., Censorship of Special Classes of Books, XII-147 pp., 1947.

263. STADLER, REV. JOSEPH NICHOLAS, J.C.L., Frequent Holy Communion.
264. SZAL, REV. IGNATIUS JOSEPH, J.C.D., The Communication of Catholics with Schismatics, XII-217 pp., 1947.
265. WAGNER, REV. URBAN STANLEY, O.F.M.Conv., J.C.D., Parochial Substitute Vicars and Supplying Priests, IX-126 pp., 1947.
266. QUINN, REV. JOSEPH, M.A., J.C.L., Documents Required for the Reception of Orders.
267. BENNINGTON, REV. JAMES CLEMENT, A.B., J.C.L., The Recipient of Confirmation.
268. BLAHER, REV. DAMIAN JOSEPH, O.F.M., A.B., J.C.D., The Ordinary Processes in Causes of Beautification and Canonization, XVI—290 pp., 1948 (printed 1949).
269. CLUNE, REV. ROBERT BELL, B.A., J.C.D., The Judicial Interrogation of the Parties, XII—142 pp., 1948.
270. COURTEMANCHE, REV. BASIL F., B.A., J.C.D., The Total Simulation of Matrimonial Consent, XX—120 pp., 1948.
271. DLOUHY, REV. MAUR JOHN, O.S.B., A.B., J.C.L., The Ordination of Exempt Religious.
272. DONOVAN, REV. JOHN THOMAS, PH.B., S.T.L., J.C.L., The Clerical Obligations of Canons 138 and 140.
273. FREKING, REV. FREDERICK W., A.B., S.T.B., J.C.D., The Canonical Installation of Pastors, XII—210 pp., 1948.
274. FULTON, REV. THOMAS B., J.C.D., Prenuptial Investigation, XII—190 pp., 1948.
275. GODLEY, REV. JAMES P., J.C.D., Time and Place for the Celebration of Mass, X—206 pp., 1948 (printed 1949).
276. KANE, REV. THOMAS A., A.B., B.S., J.C.D., The Jurisdiction of the Patriarchs of the Major Sees in Antiquity and in the Middle Ages, XII—153 pp., 1948 (printed 1949).
277. KENNEDY, REV. ANDREW A., J.C.L., The Annual Pastoral Report to the Local Ordinary.
278. KONRAD, REV. JOSEPH GEORGE, J.C.D., Transfer of Religious to Another Community, VIII—284 pp., 1948 (printed 1949).
279. KRESS, REV. ALPHONSE, J.C.L., Contumacy in Ecclesiastical Trials.
280. MCCARTNEY, REV. MARCELLUS ANTHONY, O.F.M., M.A., J.C.D., Faculties of Regular Confessors, XII—164 pp., 1948 (printed 1949).
281. MCCASLIN, REV. EDWARD PATRICK, M.A., S.T.L., J.C.L., The Division of Parishes.
282. MCELROY, REV. FRANCIS J., A.B., J.C.L., The Privileges of Bishops.
283. QUINN, REV. STEPHEN, M.S.SS.T., J.C.L., Relation of the Local Ordinary to Religious of Diocesan Approval.
284. SCHNEIDER, REV. EDELHARD LOUIS, S.D.S., M.A., J.C.L., The Status of Secularized Ex-Religious Clerics.
285. THOMPSON, REV. CHESTER J., A.B., J.C.L., The Simple Removal from Office.

286. O'Brien, Rev. Kenneth R., A.B., J.C.D., The Nature of Support of Diocesan Priests in the United States, XVI-162 pp., 1949.
287. Metz, Rev. John E., S.T.L., J.C.D., The Recording Judge in the Ecclesiastical Collegiate Tribunal, X-130 pp., 1949.
288. Reinhardt, Rev. Marion J., S.T.L., J.C.D., The Rogatory Commission, XIII—182 pp., 1949.
289. Ortega Uhiuk, Rev. Juan, S.J., J.C.L., De Delicto Sollicitationis.
290. Casey, Rev. James V., J.C.D., A Study of Canon 2222 § 1, XII-127 pp., 1949.
291. Allgeier, Rev. Joseph L., J.C.D., The Canonical Obligation of Preaching in Parish Churches, X—115 pp., 1949 (printed 1950).
292. Cahill, Rev. Daniel R., J.C.D., The Custody of the Holy Eucharist, XVI—178 pp., 1949 (printed 1950).
293. Carr, Rev. Aiden, O.F.M. Conv., S.T.D., J.C.L., Vocation to the Priesthood: Its Canonical Concept.
294. Knopke, Rev. Roch F., O.F.M., J.C.D., Reverential Fear in Matrimonial Cases in Asiatic Countries: Rota Cases, XII—112 pp., 1949.
295. Lavelle, Rev. Howard D., J.C.D., The Obligation of Holding Sacred Missions in Parishes, XVI—142 pp., 1949.
296. Mickells, Rev. Anthony B., J.C.L., The Constitutive Elements of Parishes.
297. Noone, Rev. John J., J.C.D., Nullity in Judicial Acts, X—147 pp., 1949 (printed 1950).
298. Sheehan, Rev. Daniel E., J.C.L., The Minister of Holy Communion.
299. Statkus, Rev. Francis J., J.C.L., The Minister of the Last Sacraments.
300. Cook, Rev. John P., J.C.D., Ecclesiastical Communities and Their Ability to Induce Legal Customs, XII—152 pp., 1949 (printed 1950).
301. Fazzalaro, Rev. Francis J., J.C.D., The Place for the Hearing of Confessions, X—150 pp., 1949 (printed 1950).
302. Hannan, Rev. Philip M., J.C.D., The Canonical Concept of *congrua sustentatio* for the Secular Clergy, XII—237 pp., 1949 (printed 1950).
303. Quinn, Rev. Hugh G., S.T.L., J.C.L., The Particular Penal Precept.
304. Gallagher, Rev. John F., J.C.L., The Matrimonial Impediment of Public Propriety.
305. Welsh, Rev. Thomas J., J.C.L., The Use of the Portable Altar.
306. Waters, Rev. Joseph L., S.S.J., J.C.L., The Probation in Societies of Quasi-Religious.
307. Regan, Rev. Michael J., J.C.L., Canon 16.
308. Byrne, Rev. Harry J., J.C.L., Investment of Church Funds.
309. Gallagher, Rev. Thomas V., J.C.L., The Rejection of Judicial Witnesses and Testimony.
310. Chatham, Rev. Josiah G., Ph.B., S.T.L., J.C.L., Force and Fear as Invalidating Marriage: The Element of Injustice.

311. Brown, Rev. James Victor, O.R.S.A., J.C.L., The Invalidating Effects of Force, Fear, and Fraud upon the Canonical Novitiate.
312. Duerr, Rev. Charles J., B.A., J.C.L., The Judicial Notary.
313. Gonzalez, Rev. Francisco J., O.S.A., J.C.L., De Parocho Religioso Eiusque Superiore Locali.
314. Hannon, Rev. James J., J.C.L., Holy Viaticum.
315. Sadlowski, Rev. Erwin L., J. C. L., The Sacred Furnishings of Churches.
316. Sego, Rev. Arthur A., J.C.L., Dispensation from the Interpellations.
317. Waterhouse, Rev. John M., J.C.L., The Power of the Local Ordinary to Impose a Matrimonial Ban.
318. Frein, Rev. Eugene B., J.C.L., The Discretionary Power of the Defender of the Matrimonial Bond.
319. Carton, Rev. George A., J.C.L., The Time Factor in the Gaining of Indulgences.
320. Walsh, Rev. John J., C.S.Sp., J.C.L., The Jurisdiction of the Inter-ritual Confessor in the United States and Canada.
321. Unterkoefler, Rev. Ernest L., S.T.L., J.C.L., The Presiding Judge in Matrimonial Causes of First Instance.

www.ingramcontent.com/pod-product-compliance
Lightning Source LLC
LaVergne TN
LVHW050211080826
844660LV00012B/394